BACK ROAD
DAYDREAMS

Also by **Niels Sparre Nokkentved**

Desert Wings: Controversy in the Idaho Desert
2001

A Forest of Wormwood: Sagebrush, Water and
Idaho's Twin Falls Canal Company
2008

Cover photo: Hiker heads down a former logging road
on Long Island in Willapa Bay, Washington.

All photos by the author, except where noted.

BACK ROAD DAYDREAMS

REFLECTIONS ON THE GREAT OUTDOORS

BY

NIELS SPARRE NOKKENTVED

PRINTED IN THE UNITED STATES OF AMERICA

First Edition 2010

Library of Congress Control Number: 2010903518
Back Road Daydreams: Reflections on the Great
Outdoors
Nokkentved, Niels S. 1947 –
Nonfiction, nature, outdoors, environment

ISBN: 1452812705
EAN-139781452812700

For
Freyja,
A sweet and gentle spirit.

"I arise each morning torn between the desire to improve the world and the desire to savor the world. This makes it hard to plan the day."

E.B. White (1899-1985)

CONTENTS

Acknowledgements

The vignettes in these pages were collected from newspaper columns and stories, some rewritten and edited and some combined. The pieces in Part One are from columns and stories first published in their original form in *The Olympian*, of Olympia, Washington, between May 2001 and July 2003. The dates of original publication are listed at the end of each piece. The photograph on page 41 originally appeared in a different format in *The Olympian* on October 29, 2002. I want to thank Manageing Editor Jerry Wakefield and the Olympian for permission to use the material.

The material in Part Two originally appeared in *The Times-News* in Twin Falls, Idaho, and is used with permission. The dates of publication are listed at the end of each piece.

I want to thank Vicky Runnoe and Sharon Watson for reading the manuscript, for their wise suggestions and their helpful editing.

And I want to thank William E. Brock, friend and colleague, for permission to use the photograph on the back cover.

Part One: Puget Sound

Mount Rainier, Washington

A voyage of rediscovery

In May 2001, I took a job as an outdoor writer in Western Washington and started a new chapter in my life.

For most of the previous 13 years, I had written about natural resources and environmental issues for a regional daily newspaper in southern Idaho. During those years, my writing took me deep into the deserts and mountains. I paddled lakes and rivers and camped and hiked in the Sawtooth and the Boulder-White Cloud mountains of central Idaho—an area now home to numerous wolf packs.

My new job involved writing about such outdoor adventures. It also involved writing a weekly column about outdoor activities and issues. My agenda soon evolved into an attempt to entice people to get outdoors by sharing my own simple adventures and the adventures of others. In part, I wanted to show readers that outdoor adventures don't require a lot of special equipment—other than good rain gear perhaps—or extensive expeditions to exotic places. I wanted to show that you don't have to travel to Tibet or Nepal, or even climb Mount Rainier to have a meaningful adventure. Oh, I wrote about some of those too, but satisfying and worthwhile adventures are right outside the back door.

Many of my own adventures began within a half hour of my home. Some others took a little longer, but the most important thing I learned was to just get outside—a simple walk along a stream, a farmer's field or a park path. If I had my eyes and ears open, and stopped occasionally to sniff the air and listen, adventure or a reasonable substitute was sure to find me.

One of my favorite haunts in Idaho is the high sagebrush plateau of southwestern corner of the state, where the most spectacular scenery is hidden from view to the casual observer. This part of Idaho is the largest expanse of real estate without a paved road in the lower 48 states. The sea of sagebrush offers no clue to the canyons that drop right at your feet, cutting through this all-but-uninhabited landscape. From the abrupt rim that drops eight hundred to one thousand feet, the East Fork of the Owyhee River, a silver ribbon lined with green winds below vertical ochre walls. The canyons here appear so suddenly they take my breath away the same way Mount Rainier does when it pops up around a turn in the road.

I remember one hot July afternoon in the late 1990s, sitting on a lava outcropping and looking out over the wild sagebrush landscape—a place so remote an echo would die of loneliness—my apologies to the late Ernest Hemingway. Mountain mahogany trees clumped together, as if for company, and stoic junipers, many of them older than the white settlements in this state, stand unperturbed. Purple mountains danced in the haze of distance on the horizon. The afternoon heat cut through the thin air at more than six thousand feet.

I watched as a thunderhead built from nothing and soon blotted out the sun, spreading a cast-iron curtain across the land. Heavy raindrops raised little puffs of dust on the road. Boulder-splitting lightning struck nearby. Cooling rain found the leaks in my Vietnam Era army surplus poncho and trickled down between my shoulder blades. The storm soon passed, leaving the landscape washed, and the air cooler and redolent of wet basalt, juniper and the thick sweet smell of sagebrush—a smell known locally as cowboy perfume.

On another adventure on a warm late September day in 1993 in this same area, I was on my way with three companions to a Shoshone-Paiute tribal religious ceremony at a remote desert butte. As we bounced along a set of vague tracks, we passed a group of about a half-dozen pronghorn antelope. A large buck left the group of smaller females, crossed the road behind us and came trotting up parallel to the left side of the Ford Explorer—maybe twenty yards away.

Sleek and tawny and white, shimmering in the bright high desert sun, with black markings on his head, the male might have weighed 150 pounds, standing more than four and half feet tall at the shoulder. His characteristic black horns, about a foot long, rose with forward facing tines from his forehead with the points curving in and back. His head high, eyes blazing and nostrils flared, he slowed to match our speed, stopped to mark our progress. He pranced across broken ground, keeping a wary eye on us. Suddenly he put on a burst of speed, dust flying from his hooves—only a cheetah is faster on land than the pronghorn. He turned a cut across the road a half dozen feet in front of the vehicle. About twenty yards from the road he stopped, snorted and looked back at us over his left shoulder.

It was impossible to tell whether he was showing off for the females or whether he thought the blue Explorer was a potential competitor. He watched us for a few seconds and trotted back toward the females. They all went back to grazing among the sagebrush.

But before I moved to Idaho in 1988, I had lived in western Washington for about fifteen years. The northwest corner of the state, a narrow strip of land inhabited by more than three million people, faces Puget Sound with its back against the Cascade Mountains. The mountains aren't high, maybe seven thousand to eight thousand feet in elevation, but they start basically at sea level. Large parts of the mountains are accessible from highways that cross the range and on old logging roads. But they also hold a lot of wild and rugged land accessible only on foot or horseback. So this new assignment turned out to be a voyage of rediscovery.

After I moved to Idaho, I never forgot my frequent trips on the glacier covered flanks of Mount Baker, the hours of watching birds in the Skagit River delta or the grueling hike to the top of Mount St. Helens—after it blew its top. This country west of the Cascade Mountains is as wet and hilly as the lava plains of southern Idaho are flat and dry.

Back in Washington I would come to miss some

things about Idaho—especially the smell of sagebrush. But I looked forward to visiting some of my old haunts in Washington and to discovering new ones. The woods here still hold many wild places to be explored and many adventures to be experienced. No one said it better than the late Supreme Court Justice William O. Douglas. "The mountains of the Pacific Northwest are tangled, wild, remote and high. They have the roar of torrents and avalanches in their throats," Douglas wrote in his book "Of Men and Mountains." He noted also that "the richness of life is found in adventure." In that sense I had returned to a place of unequalled richness.

In the following pages I share some of my own outdoor adventures. These stories are collected and adapted from outdoor columns and articles I have written for newspapers in the Northwest.

High Tide, Low Clouds

Craft Island, Skagit River Delta, Washington

Noting the tide

One of the greatest jobs I ever had was working for the Washington Department of Fish and Wildlife during my college days—I think it was just known as the Department of Wildlife in those days.

The job taught me a lot about birds, but I also learned to pay attention to tides—something immensely practical when you spend time outdoors along Puget Sound.

My job as a research assistant entailed about twenty hours a week of tromping around in various parts of the Skagit River Delta, about an hour north of Seattle, with a waterproof notebook, pencil and a pair of binoculars. I would take notes on any hawks, eagles or owls taking wounded or dead ducks and geese. I patrolled the edges of the tidal mud flats of Skagit Bay from LaConner to Stanwood.

The point of the study was to track lead from shotgun pellets in waterfowl and raptors that fed on dead and wounded birds. Any dead waterfowl I was supposed to turn in to the biologists who would test the livers for traces of lead.

I quickly learned to identify several birds from just a quick glance—the distinctive looping flight of the northern harrier, the soft, bullet shape and stiff wing beat of the short-eared owl. And, of course, there is no mistaking the bald eagle. One day I watched an adult eagle chase a wounded snow goose across Skagit Bay between the delta and Whidbey Island to the west. Frantic wing beats of the goose were followed closely by the powerful strokes of the eagle. They splashed down together about a half mile away. But the goose was too heavy for the eagle to lift from the water. The eagle headed back to shore with empty talons. In my binoculars, I could see the wounded goose sitting upright in the water.

Most of the delta is lined with levees to protect farmlands and the fabled Skagit County tulip fields from the ravages of tides and salt water. But one of my favorite spots was a hundred-foot-tall chunk of weathered granite, perhaps an erratic set there by a long-since melted mile-thick glacier. I dubbed it Delta Rock, but on the area USGS topographical map it is named Craft Island.

Reaching the rock required crossing the open salt marsh beyond the levees.

Early one cool fall Saturday I arrived at the end of the road on Fir Island. The tide was out, and I set out to explore the rock. My access on earlier outings had been blocked by the channels that cut through the marsh at high tide. During low water, however, it was a cinch to navigate the marsh, jumping from one high spot to another, stepping across narrow channels and tip-toeing through soggy areas.

Soon I was climbing the old granite of Craft Island, festooned with gnarled, wind-twisted pines and clad with mosses, ferns and grass. I followed a vague path that led around and up the north side of the rock. Near the top I passed below a small grove of trees and a rock outcrop. But as I rounded these, I stopped in my tracks. Not ten yards away, two young bald eagles hung in air, riding the updraft off the rise of the island's northwest side. I eased back into the shelter of the rocks and trees to a less-exposed vantage point. They seemed to take no notice of me. For several minutes, I watched them hang in the steady updraft off the face of the rock like a couple of hang-gliders. I was much too close for the binoculars to be of any use. Both eagles appeared to be second year juveniles, with speckled white bellies, probably siblings.

Suddenly they swooped off to disappear in the trees beyond the marsh.

I found a better place out of the wind and sat on a rock to enjoy the coffee and snack I had brought with me. The top of the island gives a commanding view of the tidal wetlands and estuary of the Skagit River. I could look across the shallow bay to the wooded headland of Camano Island, to the south and the shoreline of Whidbey Island to the west. But I forgot to pay attention to the incoming tide.

When I started back toward my car, the water was rising rapidly in the marsh. The nearly empty channels I had stepped across easily on my way out were filling fast. Low spots were flooded. I was in trouble. Working around the rising flood took time, and time was against me. Then the inevitable happened—cold water trickled down my ankle and spread inside my boot. I still had a long way to get to dry ground. I struggled to keep out of the water, squishing along with one wet foot. Finally a misstep got the other foot wet. I gave up worrying, and just headed straight back to my car. My failure to pay attention to the tide meant walking the last half mile wet to the knees.

But now the deeper channels were full—some of them waist deep—and that meant some detours. Only luck and a fortuitously placed log across the last deep channel kept the rest of me dry. I drove home with cold, bare feet—a lot wiser.

After that day, I never left home without a tide table in my field bag and a pair of dry socks in the car.

June 5, 2001

A dog this good . . .

I said goodbye to an old friend last week. My wife and I were in southern Idaho gathering our belongings for our move to Washington. In the rush of moving, I managed to spend a few moments at his grave in the backyard of our house in Twin Falls.

Huxley was a long-haired black dog of indistinct origins and about a hundred pounds. I rescued him from the pound, and I like to think I gave him a good life. I took him on long hikes, fed him well and let him sleep in the house.

I picked him because he was the only dog at the pound that didn't bark when I came through looking for a canine companion.

But someone had mistreated him. He was so afraid to get in my truck that I had to lift him into the back. When we got home, he was scared to come in the house; I had to coax him. He relaxed a little when I gave him an old sleeping bag to lie on.

Once we got to know each other, he was a real comfort to have around. He had a way of putting his head in my lap when he knew I was sad. He got me through some tough times, and he was a good companion during years I lived alone.

But he was no hunting dog. I took him out pheasant hunting with four friends once not long after I got him. Right away, Huxley got the scent of something and disappeared into some thick brush. A fine pheasant cock came flying out the top. All five of us blasted away. We all missed.

Poor Huxley was so startled by the barrage that he headed straight back to the pickup truck as fast as he could. I found him there a little later, underneath the truck and still shaking. It was the last time either of us went hunting.

Over time, he forgave me, but he never got over his fear of gunfire.

The Fourth of July was hell for the poor fellow.

Though he hated the water—he didn't mind wading a little—I taught him to ride in the canoe. The first time I got him into the aluminum boat, he sat there tense, claws trying to find purchase on the smooth metal hull. I thought he was going to be OK. But when we pulled away from the dock, he jumped. A couple of guys pulled him out of the water.

That dunking was enough. He never jumped out again.

After that I put his old sleeping bag in the bottom of the canoe. That put him at ease, and after a few trips he seemed to enjoy our frequent outings on the river.

But once while we were paddling near a trap-shooting

range I felt a strange vibration in the canoe. It took me a few moments to figure out it was Huxley trembling. Only when he could no longer hear the shots did the vibration stop.

Mostly, I think he loved our long hikes in the hills south of town. He would get excited when I pulled out my hiking boots. No matter where I went, climbing over impossible rocks, he would strain, dig in his claws, determined to follow me. Occasionally I had to climb down and give him a boost.

Out in the sagebrush or in woods, he never strayed far. And he never tangled with rattlesnakes. But he did tangle with a skunk—twice actually—same skunk. He got to sleep outside for a few nights until the aroma wore off.

As he got older, he slept more, our walks got slower, and he tired sooner.

Huxley died a couple of summers ago while I was away visiting my mother in Denmark. He was about as good a friend as a man can expect. I buried him in the backyard, and the dirt now has sunk a little, marking the grave.

My wife and I packed up a load of memories, along with houseplants, two cats and the replacement dog, a bright young yellow Lab named for the Viking fertility goddess, Freyja. She hasn't learned the art of canoeing yet—but she's tail-wagging eager to try.

July 3, 2001

Tranquility on the water

S hortly after I moved to Olympia in 2001, I discovered a pleasant little lake near my new home, and my wife and I occasionally took the canoe out on the shallow lake for an after-dinner outing.

The boat ramp at the north end of Chambers Lake was only ten minutes from home. Moments later we were sliding silently through the black water as we wound a slalom course between rafts of lily pads.

Chambers is actually two lakes connected by a shallow channel. It is one of the many small lakes in north Thurston County, a legacy of the glaciers that once covered much of the Puget Sound region—a mile thick in places. These little lakes offer a variety of outdoor activity—from championship bass fishing and water skiing to model boating and swimming—and for me, a few moments reverie, paddling among the water lilies, reeds and sedges.

The low sun danced across the surface, ruffled by a light northerly breeze. We glided past a house tucked into the trees of the west side of the lake, with a horse pasture facing the lake.

The unusually dry year in 2001, was evident in the low water level. The floating docks and boats at several homes along the eastern lakeshore rested on the mud at odd angles, stranded by drought.

When we set out on the lake, we could hear the noise of scurrying traffic and booming stereos, but it faded away at the far end, deadened by thick woods that gave no clue to what was beyond. Here the lake offered tranquility and respite from the rigors of the workday.

The lake shore was a primer in local bird life.

Ducks and geese, though wary of the long green vessel quietly approaching, were not spooked by our presence. In the reeds, we were greeted by the distinctive trill of male red-winged blackbirds.

We poked around among the water lilies at the far end of the lake and got scolded by a marsh wren—a tiny inquisitive bird with a big voice. A small dark bird walked across the lily pads in the deepening shadows of shoreline trees. We never did figure out what it was.

Above us, a group of starlings harassed a pair of red-tailed hawks, who tried to maintain their dignified soaring sweeps. Below the aerial combat, a flock of Canada geese soaked up the last rays of the sun on a well-nibbled pasture.

In the shallows at the mouth of the channel that in wetter years connects the east and west parts of Chambers Lake, we saw a great blue heron standing meditative, catatonic, stiletto beak poised to strike. With a prehistoric pterodactyl squawk, the large bird lifted in ungainly flight.

I nosed the canoe into the cut that connects the two parts of the lake to see how far we could get. Near the canoe, something roiled the murky water. Perhaps a large fish—I'm guessing carp. I've seen people fishing out here on this lake. Just as I mentioned how it seemed like a tropical jungle on the Amazon, a scaly, two-foot torpedo exploded from the water. It just missed landing in my wife's lap, cleared the canoe, and swam away furiously.

It was a big carp—a really BIG carp.

We reluctantly paddled for home as the sun's last traces faded from the underside of thin clouds.

July 17, 2001

The right to be eaten by bears

This is supposed to be a free country. People have a right to be eaten by bears, fall from a mountain or drown in a river.

OK, maybe that's a little harsh. But the possibility of being killed and eaten by a bear or mountain lion, falling from a high mountain trail or drowning in a raging white-water river is what makes wild country wild.

A couple of years ago, I was out for an early morning walk in the Sawtooth Mountains of central Idaho, when I came upon a fresh pile of bear scat right in the middle of the trail. It was early spring, and a light snow covered the ground. I recognized the still-steaming dark green pile as black bear poop, deposited only moments ago.

The bear was nearby in the thick brush.

As others who have come face to face with bears in the wild will attest, most bear encounters are not fatal or even result in injury. But such encounters change your perspective, sharpen your wits. You realize that you are not necessarily at the top of the food chain. My response on that May morning was not to feel threatened. Instead, I found myself paying closer attention to my surroundings, to where I was walking. Suddenly smells were stronger, colors brighter, the morning sun more intense. I was aware of the wind and subtle changes in direction.

I realized I had gone from being a visitor in the woods to being a part of the ecosystem. The presence of bears or cougars—or rattlesnakes, for that matter—has never deterred me from spending time in the woods. But it makes me think about what I'm doing, and it makes me stop and just listen.

I have never encountered a grizzly while on foot in the wild—though I've seen them from the safety of a truck cab, and I've slept in the open in grizzly country. As a kid, I once saw a mountain lion take down a deer—through my father's binoculars safely on a hillside a quarter of a mile away across the Bow River in the Canadian Rockies.

I accept that hiking and camping in wilderness, negotiating mountain trails and navigating wild rivers include a certain amount of risk even for the most careful. The reasons people do these kinds of things are as varied as the people who do them. For me, it is not a conscious choice to put myself at risk, rather risk simply sharpens the experience.

Most people don't take such risks lightly, nor should they. Only the foolish—or the young and reckless—ignore them. But the prudent carry pepper spray, line through a rapid beyond their capability, turn back short of their goal on a mountain when they're tired or the day is getting late. With a little common sense you can reduce the risk—except perhaps for bad luck or bad timing.

If all the "dangerous" wild animals were caged, the precipitous places had guardrails and the rapids were roped off, you might as well stay home and rent a video. Besides the most dangerous creatures in the woods are other humans.

All the same, I was glad I didn't run into a bear face to face that May morning.

July 24, 2001

Unbidden guests

While I lived in Olympia, I often walked in the quiet woods surrounding Saint Martin's Abbey, founded just outside Olympia by Benedictine monks in 1895. Trails wind through more than three hundred acres of open meadows and undeveloped woods of the abbey.

I rarely saw many people on the abbey grounds, but I saw and heard lots of birds. And it was close to home.

Deep in the woods the air has that sweet, spicy aroma of a Northwest Douglas-fir forest. Along the trails I sampled blackcaps and thimble berries. Most of the birds encountered—from warblers to hawks—were more often heard than seen in the thick forest canopy. Occasionally I saw black-tailed deer grazing in openings.

Just before dusk one evening, I had been trying to identify the source of a high-pitched, wheezy call. Suddenly it appeared on a low branch in a clearing. In the fading light, it looked like a black-throated gray warbler. While I tried to get a better look at the little bird, however, a larger bird lit on a branch nearby. At first I thought they were fighting, but then I realized the little warbler was feeding the larger bird. I soon identified the larger bird as a brown-headed cowbird chick, half again as big as the warbler.

I watched quietly. The chick landed on the road a few feet away and looked at me with its head turned and tilted as if to say hello. It pecked halfheartedly at gravel embedded in the asphalt and flew back up onto a low branch. It fussed when its surrogate mother arrived with a morsel of food. The forest foster mother made several more trips while I watched. Then, when she flew off again in search of yet another meal for her insatiable charge, the chick followed close behind to thickets deeper in the woods, giving voice to its hunger.

The little warbler—unwavering in its motherly instinct—had cared for a strange, large egg that hatched into a voracious baby and an unnaturally large and demanding fledgling.

Nature's ways are sometimes mysterious.

Cowbirds don't build their own nests. Instead, they lay their eggs in the nests of other birds, sometimes throwing out the eggs of the host bird. The unsuspecting host returns to the nest and hatches out the interloper's chick.

In the end it may not have made a big difference for the individual warbler. It may have been less work to raise a single, though larger, chick instead of the usual four of her own. For warblers in general, however, it means four fewer baby warblers this year, and one more bird that lays its eggs in other birds' nests.

The female cowbird apparently isn't judicious in its choice of nests, nor is she always successful. Some birds are not capable of raising the parasitic chick, other birds eject the intruder's eggs outright, and others simply abandon the violated nest. More than 150 species unwittingly have raised cowbird chicks, the majority of them songbirds. But the cowbird's success is estimated to be only about three percent.

That apparently is more than enough. The cowbird population has grown with the human conversion of forests into farms and pastures, and it now threatens several species, such as the Kirtland's warbler and the black-capped vireo.

I did not see the birds again that evening. But I returned often to wander the trails of Saint Martin's woods, to sample ripe berries and marvel at the birds.

August 7, 2001

The value of natural things

Acouple of weeks ago, chance brought a new book to my desk at work—and with it some old memories.

It was the second time a book by David James Duncan had appeared unbidden in my life. Both were enjoyable surprises. The latest book, "My Story as Told by Water," reminded me of almost forgotten days when I tried to master fly fishing. The first of Duncan's books had launched that effort many years earlier.

One day many years ago, a battered copy of Duncan's first novel, "The River Why," made its way mysteriously into my life. The romantic story of a fictional Oregon fly fisherman inspired me to take up the sport. As I look back, I wonder what it is about fly fishing that inspires such passion and eloquence.

I bought a used fly-rod and reel, some fly-line and a box of colorful flies. I studied the book a favorite uncle had written. He is a well-known fly fisherman in Europe who has started fly fishing schools there and written several books on the subject. Rod in one hand, book in the other and with a bit of pipe cleaner tied onto the leader as a practice fly, I learned how to cast to the imaginary trout lurking beneath the bushes in front of my house outside Stanwood, north of Seattle.

I learned how to read the water of the Skagit and the Stillaguamish rivers and how to set the fly gently on the water—most of the time. I also became adept at hooking various trees and shrubs—and occasionally the back of my own waders. I struggled with the art of identifying the insects hatching on the water and finding something in the fly box close enough to fool the trout. I even caught a few fish. But fly fishing never lit my hair on fire the way it did for Duncan. Perhaps I started too late in life.

Anyway, I took my learning with me to Idaho and tried it on some of the best fly-fishing waters in the state. Then one day, thigh-deep in the Wood River, in the Sawtooth National Recreation Area north of Ketchum—with central Idaho's Boulder Mountains looking over my shoulder—I realized that fly fishing just wasn't for me. Something about watching the moving water made me dizzy.

I reeled in my fly line and waded ashore. I sat for a long time trying to figure it out, watching the river, watching the wind blow clouds of pollen from the pines. I understood the magic, but that was the last time I went fly fishing.

I still find pleasure in the little magic moments that nature displays for us when we're quiet and pay attention. But whenever I hear people talk about fly fishing, a vague sense of regret rises in me like a trout to a fly. What am I going to tell my uncle?

Now Duncan, who steered me to fly fishing in the first

place, has given me an out.

In his new book—a collection of essays—he reminds us that rivers are so much more than just water, bed and banks, and that fly fishing is so much more than just "harvesting a resource." And he makes a passionate case for saving endangered Columbia-Snake River salmon.

His description of catching a wild Oregon coho—the magic that makes sense of the relentless November rains, and the true Northwest Thanksgiving feast he prepares with friends—made me long for the fly rod I sold some years ago. He carries his passion beyond fly fishing and tackles issues facing the Northwest. He delves into the moral and spiritual aspects of wild rivers, fishing and the importance of native wild salmon—an eternal promise sold for short term profit for a few who have long since moved on.

More important, however, Duncan made me realize it wasn't fish I was after; it was the opportunity to appreciate the wonders of a wild river, the life cycle of a caddis fly or the amazing nine hundred-mile migration of wild sockeye salmon from the ocean to the mountain lakes of central Idaho.

Thanks, David, for your eloquent and passionate plea for the salmon and other wild things, for lifting a quiet burden, and for helping me accept my passion for wild rivers and fish without wetting a line. You made me see the value of natural things, quite apart from my own gain, or the things I can learn from them, but for their own sake.

August 21, 2001

Time to pause and reflect

On the morning of September 11, I awoke to a phone call from my brother calling to tell me my mother had come through her abdominal surgery just fine.

And, oh yes, a jetliner had just flown into the World Trade Center, he said. I thought he was joking. Not until I got to work later in the day, did I learn it was no joke. It just seemed too outrageous to be real. A family crisis resolved but eclipsed by national events. The budding hope of recovery for my mother suddenly seemed in vain, for what would come of the day's events?

While hiking in the woods a few days later, it seemed impossible to me that life could go on, as if nature were oblivious to the tragic events of September 11. But as I walked, I began to notice what went on around me. Birds gathered, preparing for their trips south for the winter, deer and elk are preoccupied with the upcoming mating season, and small mammals were busy stocking their larders for the winter. Nature was getting ready for its annual show of color. Out of the shelter of the trees, the breeze had fall in its teeth, promises of a still-distant winter.

Fall is my favorite time of year, warm days of Indian summer with honey sunlight, the spicy air of dead leaves, misty mornings and cool nights. It is also a time of loss that brings the potential for new growth. Today, I can't walk in the woods in the fall without reflecting about personal loss. My father died in September nine years ago. Fall was his favorite time as well, and some of my best memories are of a time we shared in the Danish woods outside Copenhagen in October the year before he died. Sometimes it still makes me sad. But on this September day the memory was even more poignant. Out here in woods, then as now, I find solace, a place to contemplate my feelings and a place to sort out the events and emotions of what seems like the longest week in memory.

People long have turned to nature in troubled times— some to foil their enemies, some to find nourishment. Historian Simon Schama, in his book "Landscape and Memory," traces the long history of human connections with the natural world as a place of refuge, a place to seek solace and the roots of spirituality.

For one fellow hiker and paddler, nature is the way he connects with something bigger. Time outdoors for him is a way to reaffirm his respect for the natural world and his place in it.

A mountain climber and runner I met, spent the day after September 11 in the mountains. The pursuit required all his concentration—he could think of nothing else. At first it seemed to him he was merely escaping from events too terrible to contemplate, but getting away from those events and things in his own life allowed him to absorb the emotional impact of what had happened.

I know now that the loss and the pain in my own life have become part of who I am, like the scar on my thigh from a childhood accident that nearly took my life, like the recent tragedy will become part of what this country is. For me, grieving includes sharing the loss and pain and quiet time to contemplate and sort out deep feelings. And like the dead leaves of fall that nurture new growth, the pain and loss nurture compassion and understanding.

But today, winter is still many weeks away, and the sun still feels warm on my face.

September 18, 2001

Webbed feet, a state of mind

From the window at my desk at work, I can watch the weather roll in over the Black Hills to the west of downtown Olympia. One day earlier this year, I watched a line of approaching rain walk across town and advance up the hill toward the building. Soon the windows were streaming. And I remember that day back in August, when we set a new record for rainfall for the month—most of it came in a single day.

When I left Washington thirteen years ago, I moved to southern Idaho, a region that gets twelve inches of precipitation—in a good year. I heard lots of jokes about being from Washington and having webbed feet. I would laugh and go along with the joke.

But my feet don't look any different from anyone else's—OK, not significantly different. I don't have actual webs between my toes. Sitting back here in Washington again and watching it rain, I realize that the webbed feet thing is an attitude, not a birth defect.

Some of the wettest places in the country are in Western Washington: The average annual rainfall in the town of Forks on the west side of the Olympic Peninsula is around one hundred fifty inches—that's more than twelve feet. The rain gauge at the Lake Quinault Lodge, a few miles south of Forks, is marked in feet and tops out at sixteen.

People here typically take all that rain in stride. No one lets a little rain intrude on plans for outdoor activities. You just keep your hiking boots well-greased and carry a poncho or rain jacket in the pack—or invest in Gore-Tex. When they head outdoors, some folks simply assume it's going to rain. Then when the sun comes out it's like a bonus. In fact, sometimes it seems like people here don't know how to act outdoors when the sun comes out.

All that rain just cleans the air and makes things grow. And with proper rain gear, there's nothing like a long walk in the woods in a real downpour. Perhaps it comes naturally to me, being of Scandinavian heritage. Back in the old country people say there's no such thing as bad weather, just bad clothes. A small flask of antifreeze in the pack doesn't hurt either.

I remember one of my first outings after returning to Western Washington in spring of 2001—a long walk at the Nisqually National Wildlife Refuge in the Nisqually River delta at the southern end of Puget Sound.

I had forgotten about rain after my sojourn in southern Idaho's high desert.

Of course, it rained. And I, of course, had neglected to take the threat of rain seriously. I was about halfway around the five-mile loop when the rain started. The umbrella I carried was useless in the gusty wind. I had no choice but to keep going. Either way I was going to get wet.

Along the way I encountered a group of Boy Scouts—all properly attired in ponchos and rain suits—watching an eagle's nest across McAllister creek, formerly known as Medicine Creek. I was tempted to stop and look. But then another gust of wind blew in more rain. I pulled my hat down to fend off the wind. At least I had a good hat.

By the time I got back to the car, I was soaking wet. I learned my lesson. Like a good Scout, I always have a rain jacket and pants in the car. Now it carry them with me when I go walking—especially when it looks like rain.

October 2, 2001

Warmth, solitude in snow

Somewhere out there snow lies soft on the land, turning it from green and brown to black and white. It beckons irresistibly.

These shortening days and ever-lower freezing level mean it will soon be weather for cross-country skiing in the hills—it probably already is in the higher areas.

For some, winter snow means the rush of downhill speed over groomed slopes. Camaraderie waits at the bottom after the last run of the day, in the darkening gloom of a winter afternoon, as sun- and wind-burned faces retell the day's most exciting moments and the best runs.

And that all sounds like fun. But for me, the snow means escape from the madding crowds—be they ever so jolly. I get enough of crowds during the work week. Myself, I prefer to strap on a pair of long, skinny skis and head into the woods—to solitude and quiet to crisp, clean air, whether it's a set of well used tracks or untrammeled powder.

I close my eyes, and I'm out among the trees—with only the swish of skis and the squeak of bindings, my own breathing and the beating of my heart. When I stop for a moment, the air feels cold on my face, and I can hear the twitter of small birds—perhaps a group of kinglets or a wren, or the raucous cry of a jay, or a mountain bluebird all fluffed up against the cold.

Time to peel off a layer, take a swig of water and head deeper into solitude.

I recall winters past, working steadily up through the trees, then breaking into the open on a ridge to a snow-covered Christmas card vista. Along the way, gently falling snow makes it even quieter. When the sun breaks out, the light twinkling on snow crystals nearly blinds me.

A cold wind, driving snow across the ridge, keeps the stop brief. I turn back into the trees, savoring the ride down hard-earned hills.

And then there's the inevitable spills. Falling in deep snow is no laughing matter—OK, I admit, I have looked pretty silly trying to get back up.

Once, trying to right myself, I put out my hand and it promptly disappeared up to my shoulder. I tried to stand but sank to my hips in the dry powder. It's a wonder I'm not still there.

Another time, I shoved my pole into the snow to push myself back up. When I pulled up my pole after righting myself, the basket at the end was missing—caught on a branch in a six-foot drift. Back down to dig it out.

I definitely prefer not falling, but that won't keep me home.

Nor does the cold.

One nice thing about cross-country skiing is that, even on those cracking cold days of deep winter, it keeps you warm without ever working hard. And at the end of the day, cheeks red with cold, wind and exertion, a well-earned rest and maybe a cup of hot chocolate by a warm fire awaits.

November 13, 2001

A Writer's Dilemma

Lava tube beneath Mount St. Helens, Washington

Paying to play

People in the West are lucky. So many places of incomparable beauty are still available on our public lands, places where we can hike, ski, camp, fish or hunt—or just sit and watch the clouds.

These lands belong to all of us, and they are one of this country's greatest assets.

How do you place a value on floating a pale morning dun on a gin-clear stream to dance with a Yellowstone cutthroat trout at the end of a slender length of fly line; or on crunching through fallen leaves, frost still hanging in the dawn, drawn by the high resonant bugling of a bull elk in rut?

What is a bighorn sheep worth, peering from a precarious rock ledge in a landscape open and seemingly endless? Who knows the value of forests deep and dark that hide the intimate relationships linking the spotted owl, the northern flying squirrel and the mighty Douglas fir—or wild rivers once filled with salmon, undaunted in their effort to return to native streams to spawn?

These things are priceless, but public lands are not free.

Congress passed the federal recreation fee demonstration program—fee-demo for short—in 1997. The act passed at the urging of a recreation industry lobbyist, as a rider slipped into other legislation, without any debate. The U.S. Forest Service started charging fees to park at some of the most popular trail heads.

Some people hate having to pay recreation fees on public lands; others grudgingly pay up.

I hate 'em.

I guess I got spoiled living in Idaho with its wide open spaces. Most of the state's vast tracts of public land are open to recreation. Most places I went I found good hiking trails—or good hiking and no trails—with nobody else on them. No parking lots, no toilets, no people, no fees.

One drawback was that I often had to clear away the cow pies to set up my tent.

In Western Washington things are a lot different. There are lots of good hiking trails and places to camp here too. No cow pies, but a lot more people. Just about anywhere you want to go, however, you have to dig out your wallet.

Environmental author and educator Michael Frome notes correctly that charging recreation access fees on public lands turns a walk in nature into a commercial transaction. I say the transaction cheapens the experience.

The fees pay for a variety of things, but mostly they cover trail and trail head maintenance. And with more of us using the outdoors, the need for maintenance is growing. Some people support recreation fees because they help to pay for amenities used primarily by outdoor recreationists. But one thing that really bothers me is that some who profit from using public lands get a lot of help from the taxpayers. Hikers and campers don't profit. As taxpayers we already pay for a variety of public land programs.

For $5, I can park at a public land trail head for one day.

For $5, a rancher can feed one cow and her calf for three and a half months on public land. Ranchers pay about $1.50 a month for one cow and her calf to graze on public land. But it costs taxpayers an additional $6 or more per month to administer grazing programs.

For $5, a miner can buy an acre of public land under an 1872 mining law. Hard rock miners pay no royalties on the precious metals they dig out of public lands. They can patent the land around the mine for $5 an acre. But in many cases when the mine plays out, they just walk away, leaving the taxpayer with the cleanup bill. Some of the nation's most popular resorts are at least partly on such patented lands.

The Forest Service loses millions on the sale of timber from public lands. In 1998, the agency reported that timber sales lost about $126 million, according to the General Accounting Office. Some people note that the timber sale program leaves roads used by outdoor recreationists.

Perhaps. But those who profit from public land resources also should bear the cost if taxpayers who own the land are expected to pay just to go for a walk.

I'm not advocating against all recreation fees. But I think they should be considered in context. The government has gotten good at converting public land assets into private wealth. Meanwhile trout disappear, wildlife habitat is cut and winter range overgrazed, salmon are dammed to extinction and spawning streams silted in by unsound livestock management and logging practices—all subsidized at taxpayer expense. And then the government wants those same taxpayers to pay to use these overexploited public lands.

The trouble with fees is they may encourage some land managers to make decisions based on what will bring in more money, not necessarily what's best for the land or for us who own it.

I'd rather pay a pinch more in taxes and have the government spend the money where it's needed than to fork over every time I want to go for a walk. I guess, like cow pies in camp, recreation fees take some getting used to. Except that when cow pies dry out, they burn pretty well.

February 12, 2002

Reservations? In wilderness?

You know things are getting too crowded when you need reservations to camp in a wilderness area.

I learned recently that some wilderness areas in the Olympic National Park, on Washington's Olympic Peninsula, are so popular that campers have to make reservations—well in advance for the best spots.

Scenery is good, but to me wilderness is about solitude, quiet, getting away from humanity. If I have to elbow my way to a good camp spot, it's not so different from the crowds I have to deal with every day.

I realize the reservation system is the park's way of trying to limit the number of people that visit particular areas to protect the park's natural resources. Somewhere between one or two other campers and thousands, a place ceases to be true wilderness.

In addition to reservations, sleeping on the ground is no longer free in the wilderness of the Olympic National

Park. The entrance fee is $10 per vehicle—good for a week; a wilderness camping permit registration fee costs $5; a wilderness camping fee is $2 per person per night; and the park recommends a bear-proof food canister, which it will loan you—for a $3 donation.

All that adds up to $20—just for one person to sleep on the ground in the wilderness for one night. Granted, the subsequent nights cost only an additional $2 each for up to a week. Still.

Hiking into the park from an Olympic National Forest trail head would cost about the same. The Forest Service charges $5 per day to park at most trail heads. The two days worth needed to spend one night camping would cost $10. You would still have to pay for the camping permit, fee and bear-proof canister in the Olympic National Park wilderness.

So if you need reservations and it costs $20 for the first night can it really qualify as wilderness—even if Congress says so?

To me, wilderness is a place where nature is intact, where the land still looks like I'm the first human being to set foot here. It's a place where there are no guardrails, no guarantees, no admission fees, and where it doesn't cost anything to sleep on the ground—a place where wits are more important than wealth and where cell phones don't work. Wilderness is a place people drown in rivers or get caught in avalanches or eaten by bears. A place where people might not find you if you get lost, and you might die. A place that reminds us that we are a part of nature, not just spectators with reserved seats.

OK, so I'm an idealist, but that's the way it should be—if you're going to call it wilderness. Unfortunately most wilderness areas have been trammeled by human intrusion. Even the largest chunk of designated wilderness in the lower 48 states—the Frank Church River-of-No-Return Wilderness in the central mountains of Idaho—is dotted with private ranches and airstrips. That's right, you can hire a pilot to fly you to a remote airstrip for a week or a weekend of camping and fishing in pristine mountain streams, and then fly out again.

Even in Idaho they call that wilderness. I don't know if you need reservations, but if you do, it seems to me more like just a primitive recreation area. It's nice that so many people enjoy the outdoors so much that in the most popular areas, you need reservations to find a camp spot.

Thankfully, there are still a few places that provide a wilderness experience—without reservations or fees. But you have to hunt for them, and many are in unexpected places not officially recognized as "wilderness."

April 19, 2002

Nature's surprises

On a late fall weekend in 2001, I took a group of house guests to Woodard Bay, a nature preserve on Puget Sound just north of Olympia, in hopes of seeing harbor seals and birds.

We weren't disappointed.

Once the site of a busy log dump, the Woodard Bay reserve—established in southern Puget Sound in the late 1980s—is a sanctuary for nature. Today it's home to a variety of birds, harbor seals, river otters, bald eagles and an important great blue heron rookery.

That day the bay was full of ducks, and the harbor seals were hauled out on the log booms, making the kind of obscene sounding noises that delight fifth-graders. But the real treat perched in the top of a nearby fir tree. A pair of bald eagles were so close we didn't need binoculars to watch them. We were from far enough away, though, that we didn't disturb them as they preened themselves.

But things were not always so peaceful here.

The six-hundred-acre reserve encompasses maturing second-growth forest, the waters of Woodard and Chapman bays and a rich history that spans from American Indian use to settlement in the 1850s and Puget Sound's logging era.

A logging railroad brought timber from South Puget Sound forests across Woodard Bay on an old wooden trestle—now closed to the public. The trains ran onto a pier in Henderson Inlet across the mouth of Chapman Bay, where they dumped the logs into the water to be gathered into rafts and floated to lumber mills in Everett far to the north.

Mosses, ferns and trees—to say nothing of the microscopic agents of rot—are taking over this former log dump. The railroad trestle is slowly disintegrating. The dilapidated railroad pier is home to a colony of rare bats.

Outside the pier, harbor seals find a place to rest on what's left of the old log booms. Eagles nesting in the fir trees here, seem oblivious as time and creeping rot take their toll. The natural processes will eventually obliterate the human history here.

One Saturday in 2002, Washington state officials gathered at the Woodard Bay Natural Resource Conservation Area to mark the opening of public facilities and interpretive signs. While the facilities are a nice addition and help explain the natural and human history that intersect on this spit of land, nothing state officials or anyone else could do here would improve upon the natural assets.

Even on a gray day—or perhaps especially on a gray day—Woodard Bay shows off the region's assets. And everywhere, nature is slowly reclaiming the evidence of former uses and abuses here.

But this is a nature preserve—not a recreation area.

Chapman Bay is closed to boaters, to protect nesting eagles and the heron rookery. And the waters of Woodard Bay are closed from Labor Day to April 1 to protect wintering waterfowl. Pigeon guillemots and cormorants roost here, and a purple martin colony has been reestablished in the area.

A short distance from the entrance off Woodard Bay Road, a mile-long loop trail wanders beneath a cathedral canopy of big leaf maple, western red cedar, Douglas fir and hemlock. Winter wrens and kinglets serenade a solitary hiker. Mink are active during the day along the water's edge.

It is a good place to come and learn about the area's abundant wildlife—175 species of birds have been recorded here. "It's a place to come and be," area manager Leslie Durham said. "It's a good place to contemplate nature."

That sentiment fits a lot places outdoors. And as an old friend is fond of reminding me: "Mother Nature bats last." Nowhere I have been is that more evident than at Woodard Bay, where you can see her in action, batting cleanup.

May 10, 2002

A walk is its own reward

I think it got up to 94 degrees—unheard of in June in Puget Sound—warm, bright sunshine and a light breeze.

It was about the nicest day since I moved to Washington more than a year earlier. Given the day, I decided to forego my usual workout at the downtown YMCA, and instead go for a hike along Capitol Lake just below the state Capitol building, as did a lot of others that day.

The lake is formed by a weir that holds back the Deschutes River, where it runs into Puget Sound, and keeps salt water out of the lake.

It's becoming almost a habit for me on nice days. I never pass up a chance to get outdoors, and as often happens I was rewarded for my effort. I went as far as half my allotted time would get me and turned around. But as I approached the mouth of Percival Creek, a small tributary that enters Percival Cove on the west side of the upper end of Capitol Lake, I noticed about a dozen crows making a fuss over something in the water.

Something large, dark and feathered rose from the creek and took flight with the squawking crows in close pursuit. As soon as it cleared the brush that lines the creek, I could see clearly that it was an adult bald eagle with an eight- to ten-inch trout in its talons. The crows appeared to be trying to make the eagle drop the fish. The eagle was easily more that twice the size of any of the crows. But to defend itself it would have to let go of its prize.

A true dilemma.

But determined wing beats lifted the big bird, trying its best to ignore the pesky crows. The eagle gained altitude and speed, with the crows in hot pursuit above the water.

One by one the crows gave up the chase.

The eagle headed out over Capitol Lake toward the trees below the dome of the Capitol—white head and tail against a seriously blue sky—trailed by black wings flashing above the ruffled water.

Soon the last of the black stragglers gave up and broke off the chase.

Crows have neither the beaks nor the talons to capture and kill prey as large as a trout. But the opportunistic feeders are savvy enough to cooperate and often rely on such gang tactics to steal the prey of others.

Even eagles will eat what others have killed rather than hunt their own.

More than once driving back roads, I have come upon an eagle tearing into road kill too big to carry off, or devouring waterfowl mangled by inept hunters.

And eagles flock to the easy pickings of dead and dying spawned-out salmon.

This time the eagle won. It soon disappeared in the woods along the east side of the lake, presumably to devour its prize or perhaps feed it to nestlings. The crows went back to prey they could catch on their own in the north part of the lake—perhaps scavenging discarded French fries.

And I went back to work refreshed—whatever had been on my mind when I set out, was now forgotten. OK, so I was about ten minutes late getting back to work.

June 21, 2002

Adventure clears the mind

There's a photo on my cubicle wall of a friend named Orville and me, sharing a cup of coffee on a frosty September morning in the early 1990s along the South Fork of the Snake River in eastern Idaho.

For me the picture captures the camaraderie that is the essence of outdoor adventures. It illustrates a bond, intangible as the mist rising from the river that grows from shared adventure. And it reminds me why I looked at the familiar world with new eyes after I returned from that trip and others like it.

It was my first trip down a large moving river, and I paddled an overloaded aluminum canoe. I lacked the experience to give proper directions to my paddling partner up in the bow. In short, we had set ourselves up for disaster—I'm still surprised that things didn't go worse. Orville and I and five others launched our boats at the foot of Palisades Dam in eastern Idaho near the Wyoming border and headed down the South Fork of the Snake River.

The first day, except for a couple of nervous moments and one minor spill, went well enough as we drifted through the scenic Swan Valley. Late in the day my paddling partner and I found ourselves in a side-channel, panicked and hopelessly fighting the current. Despite our efforts, however, the channel eventually got us where we wanted to go—albeit with sore shoulders and tired backs. Chagrined we met the rest of our party and camped that night on a wide bank under cottonwoods in the wilderness along the South Fork. September was starting its magic, turning the high-country foliage golden.

The river flows through one of the few remaining intact western riparian forests in Idaho, dominated by mature black cottonwood and thickets of coyote willow. Bald eagles floated overhead. A moose cow and calf at water's edge cast us a wary glance. Drift boats with fly fishermen slid past on the current—better than three miles per hour. A hissing propane cooked up a big pot of pasta for our party of seven, to say nothing of the two dogs.

With a mist rising from the river in the frosty morning of the second day, Orville and I shared a cup of espresso, made on the propane stove. The rest of the world was not yet awake, and stillness was our only other companion.

But even here in this seemingly pristine wilderness, the Snake is anything but wild. It is termed a working river by those who profit from it and harness its power for irrigation and hydroelectric power. The river flow depends on the amount of water released by the Bureau of Reclamation from Palisades Dam where our journey started. And that depends largely on how much water irrigators need. In September, the river typically runs at seven thousand cubic feet per second—more than three million gallons per minute.

The Snake River is born of melting snow on the Yellowstone plateau in Wyoming at 9,800 feet above sea level. From one end of a small lake that straddles the continental divide in Yellowstone National Park, water flows into the Yellowstone River drainage, the Missouri and the Mississippi to the Gulf of Mexico. From the other end of the lake, a trickle joins other rills to become the second largest river in the West, the Snake River. It flows south out of the park and then west in a broad arc across southern Idaho. It turns north and forming the Oregon-Idaho border it runs through Hells Canyon to Lewiston, where it turns west again to join the Columbia River to the Pacific Ocean. The average annual flow is about 35 million acre-feet, more than twice the flow of the Colorado River. On its 1,038-mile journey, the Snake River drops about 9,500 feet in elevation. When it reaches the Columbia River in south-central Washington the Snake has dropped to 340 feet.

On its way, the river provides water for irrigation and for hydropower generation; it flushes away sewage effluent and agricultural runoff. It also provides a lot of habitat for fish and wildlife in its waters and along its banks. And it provides places of refuge from the industrial world that it supports. Anglers find places to pursue wily trout, and canoeists find challenging rapids and shaded camping spots along it shores. It can be calm and soothing in some places, while in others the waters are so turbulent that only experts, or the foolhardy, venture out on them in kayaks or rafts, and sometimes they die.

As we floated through riffles and placid pools, the foothills of the Teton Mountains on the right dipped their rugged toes right into the river. On the left, rolling hills hinted at the vast Eastern Snake River Plain that cuts a wide swath across southern Idaho. But with the end of the trip in sight, circumstance found us on the right side of the river. It turned out to be the wrong side. Just upstream from the take-out, a rip-rap dam blocked the river. The only navigable passage was near the left bank, and the river suddenly seemed a hundred yards wide. The current drove us inexorably toward the rocks. We would have to paddle across the current to reach the opening head on. I envisioned the dented, broken canoe floating downstream, gear bobbing in the water and myself mangled on the rocks.

We paddled like we were possessed. My last paddle stroke hit rock and air. We had cleared the rocks— barely. We turned straight into the four-foot drop and bounced through a standing wave to quiet water below without getting us wet.

The incident added a last-minute charge of adrenaline to a beautiful trip. For me, the risks that come with outdoor adventures sharpen the experience, and add to the sense of camaraderie.

After returning from the South Fork canoe trip, things I took for granted suddenly had meaning—familiar things didn't look quite the same. But it was me that had changed, not the world. At the very heart of the experience is the direct focus on the moment. Nothing matters except what you're doing and what's happening around you. On the river, it's reading the water and responding to hazards or steering through the middle of the rapid, keeping the boat pointing downstream. Sometimes that demands all your concentration and effort, and that's part of the attraction. But then the smooth water that follows, gives us time to reflect on the natural beauty of the wilderness we passed through. Or there's the well earned rest at the end of the trip and time to reflect on the marvels of the journey.

At the end of the trip, practical matters intrude again—loading the boat, stowing the gear, the long trip home. And always when I get home from a few days in the back country, I marvel at the magic of hot water gushing from a pipe sticking out of the wall—soothing tired muscles. And then in the evening there's recounting the adventure over a glass of wine and a good meal.

That's about as good as it gets. Skål!

July 19, 2002

Peregrine falcons recover

In the bright sunlight, a mist rose from sand left wet by a receding tide. A flock of sanderlings fed along the beach, little legs scurrying as they raced ahead of an incoming wave.

Shorebirds, hundreds of them, intently probed the mud for tiny animals at the water's edge on the leeward side of the Ocean Shores Peninsula that separates the northern bay of Grays Harbor from the Pacific Ocean. Suddenly the flock, mostly sanderlings, and a small group of marbled godwits, rose as one and dissipated. The moment was a testament to the recovery effort for the peregrine falcon that had been clinging to the cliff edge of extinction.

In the fall of 2001, on an outing with Washington birder and author Bob Morse, I saw my first peregrine falcon in action. Bob spotted it first, and then I saw the feathered gray projectile, wings tucked, that dove into the midst of the flock, less than a quarter mile away.

The six-mile long Ocean Shores Peninsula, laced with canals and lakes and the Pacific beaches to the west and the extensive estuary of Grays Harbor to the east, is one of the best places in Washington for watching birds, especially shorebirds. Most of the 365 bird species found on the Pacific Coast can be seen here. Standing on the jetty at the south end of the peninsula one day, I watched four crook-necked brown pelicans glide by just over the water. I counted sooty shearwaters, cormorants, loons, grebes, auklets, a variety of ducks, terns and gulls.

Shorebirds by the tens of thousands congregate here, and they attract more than just bird watchers. Birds of prey find good hunting here as well. This is one of three areas in Washington where peregrines are winter residents. The other two are Samish Flats and Sequim, both on the Puget Sound.

Once a rare sight, peregrine falcons teetered on the brink of extinction. But they have made a stunning comeback—with some human help. A ban on the use of the pesticide DDT, captive breeding and reintroduction programs, and the protection of nest sites have helped bring the bird back over the past twenty years. Falcons are sensitive to DDT, which results in thin and fragile eggshells.

By 1970, the species was wiped out east of the Mississippi and down to thirty-nine known pairs in the West. The peregrine was included on the federal list of endangered species. In Washington, biologists found just five peregrine falcon pairs in 1980, when the state listed it as endangered.

Tom Cade of Cornell University, using falcons

borrowed from falconers, successfully raised twenty young falcons in 1973. He released the first captive-bred falcons the following year. Cade's efforts led to the formation of the Peregrine Fund and the creation of the World Center for Birds of Prey in Fort Collins, Colorado. The two joined and moved to Boise, Idaho, in 1984. At the time, no one knew whether a recovery effort would work. Eventually four thousand falcons were raised in captivity and released in twenty-eight states.

Peregrine falcons still are plagued with thinner than normal eggshells—the result of eating prey that winter in countries where DDT still is used, from pesticide residue at breeding grounds, or from illegal use of the chemical in the United States.

The falcons also lack suitable nesting sites close to food sources and free from human disturbances. Peregrine falcons occur nearly worldwide. They usually nest on cliff ledges and lay three or four eggs in April. They catch smaller birds—usually on the wing. Hunting territories may extend to a radius of twelve to fifteen miles.

The birds are sixteen to nineteen inches long, with a long tail and pointed wings that span thirty-nine to forty-two inches. They weigh about two pounds and live up to seventeen years.

And they can dive at more than two hundred miles per hour.

In winter and fall, peregrines spend much of their time foraging in areas with large shorebird or waterfowl concentrations, such as Grays Harbor on the Washington coast. The birds are no longer considered endangered. They are considered a sensitive species and protected under a migratory bird treaty.

And they are still a rare sight.

That day, the peregrine that Bob and I had been watching came away with empty talons. Unaware of our presence, it perched on a piece of driftwood, maybe a football field away, while it rested for its next attempt.

It would have plenty of opportunities to try again, as the birds soon began drifting back along the shore.

August 2, 2002

Contemplating the universe

It's mind boggling, really, when you stop and think about all the stars in the sky. But to really see the stars, get out of town.

No place is better for stargazing than open country far from town—specially high on a mountain or on a high desert plateau. Anytime you're going camping, take some time to look up at the stars and ponder the universe or just marvel.

Sometime in the early 1990s, I stopped to camp in the desert in southwestern corner of Idaho near the Oregon border. It was dark by the time I reached the campsite.

While I was pulling tent and sleeping bag out of the car, I noticed how dark the sky was and all the stars. I looked up at an astounding array of stars. I dispensed with the tent, and unrolled my sleeping bag on the ground-cloth and lay there looking up.

This was a good vantage point. The dry desert air,

above 5,000 feet elevation and miles from the nearest electric light, offered little interference.

In a place like this, with a good spotting scope mounted on a tripod, you can easily see the four largest of Jupiter's moons and the distinctive bands that cross the giant planet's middle. You can pick out the rings of Saturn.

Those pinpoints of light came at me from an incomprehensible distance measured by how far light travels in a year.

At the speed of light, 186,000 miles per second, and with 31.5 million seconds in a year, that pencils out to roughly 5.859 trillion miles in a year. It might as well be forever.

As I lay there, I realized I was looking back at light that was thousands or even millions of years old. The light that twinkled at me, had left some of those stars thousands of years ago.

Perhaps on some planets circling distant stars, civilizations had risen, thrived and died out again since the light I saw had left their sun. Some of the stars may have gone out long ago, but the light is only just getting here.

The distance, the vastness of the galaxy and the universe, is just incomprehensible.

I noticed for the first time that the Milky Way really spans the entire sky, from horizon to horizon. And it really is a distinctive swath of stars all the way across the sky—as if someone had swung a giant paint brush, splattering speckles of white against the night sky.

I saw the small bright point of a satellite, or perhaps the international space station, moving steadily from the southwest to the northeast until it suddenly faded from my sight.

A friend once suggested, while we were on our backs looking up at the same night sky somewhere in the Sierra Nevada of eastern California, many years earlier and in a similar manner, perhaps we humans are just the universe's way of looking at itself.

I drifted off to sleep pondering the meaning of it all.

August 16, 2002

Changes

What have we learned? Has anything really changed in the year since September 11, 2001? The sun still comes up, the rain still comes down. The grass grows tall, and apples ripen. The tide comes in, and it goes back out. And my mother recovered from an operation to remove a tumor from her large intestine.

The salmon are trying to come back upstream, and the bears are gorging on berries in preparation for hibernation. Even as leaves turn color and start to fall, trees are making buds that will eventually become new leaves next spring.

Nature never looks back. And that's reassuring in this troubled time.

On late summer days, it becomes easier to find some quiet and solitude on a trail outdoors. And in the quiet of the outdoors—a spicy after-rain aroma permeates the air—I find time to digest and reflect on the past year.

Despite the media blitz telling us how things have changed since last September, I realize that in the larger scheme of things the world hasn't changed. That particular day was a mind-numbing reminder of how things are in the real world.

Before the World Trade Center, there were bombs at an embassy and a marine barracks in Beirut; at embassies in Kenya and Tanzania; PanAm 103 blown out of the sky over Lockerbie, Scotland; someone blew a hole in the side of the U.S. Navy destroyer USS Cole; and a military housing complex in Dhahran, Saudi Arabia was bombed.

Then April 19, 1995, some lunatic blew up the Alfred P. Murrah building in Oklahoma City, and before that there was the first attack on the World Trade Center in 1993.

That all makes me wonder what we've learned since last September. It makes me wonder about our oil-soaked policy in the Middle East, about how people in other countries see us, how we treat them, and how we treat each other.

I don't think much has changed. Human power struggles come and go. Carnivores kill and eat grazers in mind-numbing carnage. The wind whips up falling leaves, and signal the approach of my favorite time of the year. Summer is heading south and leaving some regrets. But fall and winter don't bring an end, they bring rebirth and rejuvenation.

Fall and winter also bring cross-country skiing, snow-shoeing, and for the really adventurous, snow camping, as well as some great winter hikes in rain-soaked Puget Sound lowland forests.

By next spring young salmon will hatch, and trout will start biting as the alders begin to leaf out. Gray whales will make their annual pilgrimage to rich northern waters, and the sage grouse begin their fascinating early morning mating dance on the same lek they've used for years—probably the same one their ancestors used.

They never look back.

Come spring, I'll wipe the winter's dust from my hiking boots. For me, sorrow and loss are personal and very much a part of life. My favorite hiking partner— though we shared far too few hikes—died 10 years ago this month. An unexpected rain took us by surprise the last time we walked together. We both got soaked.

And a lot of rain has fallen since then.

Just a few days ago, hiking on a mountain trail overlooking Mount St. Helens, I realized for the moment none of this mattered. What mattered was that my rain poncho was back in the car, and rain clouds were building, piling up against the mountains.

September 20, 2002

Fall memories

The day dawned cool, with the sun burning off a morning mist. That unmistakable dead-fish low-tide aroma hung in the still, humid air.

No mistaking it. Fall had arrived.

Even as the rain came down, the memories of recent spectacular late-summer days in Puget Sound remained. The day before the rains, dry leaves crunched underfoot. Pileated woodpeckers returned to eat the bright red berries on the Pacific dogwood tree in my backyard.

Golden ash trees and blood red maples are washed in warm, lazy sunlight. On this particular day, my jacket quickly became too warm. It was the kind of dreamlike day that reminded me of another fall day, now long gone as well.

I had set out for a day of hunting pheasants with a friend in southern Idaho. We walked the dusty, weed covered banks of dry irrigation ditches in our shirtsleeves on an uncommonly warm early November Sunday with an impossibly blue sky. My friend's young springer spaniel, full of uncontained enthusiasm, bounded ahead, making sure we would never have to raise our shotguns.

I had left my own non-hunting dog at home. He didn't understand, but I reassured him he was better off. Huxley hated guns and other loud noises.

Craig and I didn't really care much about our chances to shoot anything. The day just demanded to be enjoyed. We lapped up the golden fall sunlight as we waded through tawny grasses, through rustling corn stalks and dusty green sagebrush, raising puffs of light tan dust in the track we walked.

We had some good conversation and a long walk, with the weight of the double-barrel, 16-gauge shotgun and a handful of shells in my pocket for ballast—an armed hike. Every so often my friend would have to stop and call his pup to keep her in sight.

Rough-legged hawks had come down from their summer place to the north to join the red-tail hawks, hunting for ground squirrels and voles in harvested grain fields. Turkey vultures soared on their unsteady wings. A pair of ducks winged by, bound for wetlands along one of the irrigation ditches that lace this landscape. And a ragged string of Canada geese passed overhead far to the north.

But we didn't see even a single pheasant—not that it mattered. We regretted only that the day was over as we re-cased the shotguns back at his house with daylight waning.

Perhaps it was time to give up pheasant hunting or move to Iowa, I mused. My friend later moved to northern

Minnesota. I sold my shotgun and moved to Washington. And lining up to shoot pen-raised pheasants on the day they are released, you can't really call hunting.

I don't miss the weight of the shotgun—now I carry a field guide and binoculars instead. On days like that, though, it doesn't matter what I do, as long as I can do it outdoors. But rain started falling Thursday, reminding me to keep the poncho in my old green field bag.

October 4, 2002

Adversity inspired passion

On a recent visit to a used book store, I stumbled onto a book by one of my favorite outdoors writers, former Supreme Court Justice William Orville Douglas. The volume included descriptions of the Washington coast as fresh today as they were forty years ago when he wrote them.

Douglas is known for his eloquence, not just in court opinions, but also in his books about his outdoor adventures. When I read his description of frying a freshly caught trout over a campfire, I can smell it cooking and hear it sizzling. He wrote with clarity of vision, a reverence for the natural world and a passion for the outdoors in general and the Pacific Northwest in particular.

"The wildest, the most remote and, I think, the most picturesque beach area of our whole coastline lies under a pounding surf along the Pacific Ocean in the state of Washington. It is marked as Cape Alava on the north and the Quillayute River on the south. It is a place of haunting beauty, of deep solitude," he wrote in "My Wilderness: The Pacific West," in 1960.

He may not find the solitude on a summer weekend today, but the wild beaches of the Olympic Peninsula's west side look much as they did when Douglas first visited them in the late 1950s, in part because of his passionate words in the defense of wild nature to keep them that way—unchanged but for the effects of the time and the tides that erase the footprints of the thousands that now hike the wild beaches.

This book should be required reading for all Northwest residents—or at least for anyone who enjoys the outdoors.

Douglas did not come to his love of the outdoors easily. He was born in Minnesota in 1898, and his family moved to Yakima shortly thereafter. Polio afflicted the young Douglas. His doctor wasn't sure Douglas would survive. Sickly and uncomfortable with physical activity, he was urged by a friend to hike the nearby Cascade foothills to strengthen his legs and lungs. At first, the hikes brought more discomfort. But he didn't give up, and gradually his spindly legs grew stronger.

Douglas eventually became an avid hiker, at times covering 30 miles or more in a day. He wrote of his adventures in the rugged Cascade Mountains and about the people he met there who, like Douglas, were enriched by their lives outdoors.

"I learned early that the richness of life is found in adventure. Adventure calls on all the faculties of mind and spirit. It develops self-reliance and independence. Life then teems with excitement. But man is not ready for adventure unless he is rid of fear. For fear confines him and limits his scope. He stays tethered by strings of doubt and indecision and has only a small and narrow world to explore," he wrote in "Of Men and Mountains," in 1950.

Douglas was appointed to the Supreme Court in 1939 by President Franklin D. Roosevelt. He served more than thirty-six and a half years—longer than any other justice—until a stroke led him to retire in 1975.

Douglas died in 1980 at eighty-two. But his legacy lives on in his landmark Supreme Court opinions that reflect his respect for nature and, more important to me, in his books about his outdoor adventures.

And I can't think of a more fitting memorial than the William O. Douglas Wilderness east of Mount Rainier, the spectacular wild lands between the Naches and Tieton rivers where he hiked as a young man to overcome a crippling disease, where he learned his passion for the outdoors, and where he learned to shed his fear.

October 18, 2002

Beneath the volcano

Absolute, total darkness, chilly and damp against my face, obscured everything—total isolation—flashlights feeble and ineffective against the pervasive subterranean gloom. Infinite blackness.

On a sunny day in October, I headed into the black depths of the lava tubes on the southwest side of Mount St. Helens in Washington state with a local outdoor group, the Olympia Mountaineers.

We picked our way among tumbled, broken rock that led under the forest floor, into the dark cave opening—darker than any midnight after only a short distance. Then the cave floor dropped abruptly about twelve feet. A steel chain ladder bolted to the rock offered the only way down. Beyond that, walking was easy on the sandy cave floor—but only for a short distance. Jumbled boulders blocked the way. Here part of the cave roof had collapsed. Some tried climbing over; others tried crawling under. The easiest way seemed to be to drop down a six-foot chute and then squeeze under the rocks on hands and knees, but this was not for claustrophobics.

For visitors to the Mount St. Helens National Volcanic Monument, an extra day to explore the lava tubes offers a unique perspective on the volcano. The longest and most accessible is Ape Cave, stretching to about two miles. The Gifford Pinchot National Forest offers guided tours in Ape Cave, which logs about 130,000 to 185,000 visitors annually.

But for those thirsting for adventure, the lesser-known lava tubes a little south of Ape Cave offer plenty. These caves are shorter but more rugged. And unlike the guided tours in Ape Cave, explorers are on their own in Lake and Ole's caves. Exploring these caves requires the skills to navigate with a map and compass—and adventurers who aren't claustrophobic or afraid of the dark.

But don't go alone. In fact, it is better to go with someone who has some experience in caves. It can be scary down there in addition to disorienting. If you lose your light, you have to find your way out strictly by feel.

The lava tubes at Mount St. Helens were formed almost two thousand years ago, when tongues of lava flowed from vents in the flanks of Mount St. Helens. As the outer crust of the lava began to cool and harden, the still-viscous molten rock inside continued to flow, eventually draining the tube and leaving the solid outer walls.

Other flows added complexity to the now-empty passages by melting and joining parts of earlier tubes. Subsequent flows in some tubes have left lateral ridges along the sides. Heat from the still-flowing lava partly melted the ceiling in places, forming "lava-sicles," hanging from the cave roof.

Eventually, the lava cooled, soil began to form, and plants returned to the rocky landscape. Trees returned, too, sending roots into the soil through cracks among the rocks. In a few places where the tubes are close to the surface, weak rock has collapsed, revealing the caves beneath.

A short walk from the trail head, Lake Cave starts among the trees as an unremarkable sinkhole maybe twenty feet across. But nothing on the surface hints at the extensive cave that opens beneath the ground.

The cave runs for a little more than a mile and descends about 225 feet along the way. It was discovered in 1958 by a party of the St. Helens Apes, the same group of young outdoorsmen who first explored Ape Cave in 1952.

On this day, each of the twelve members of the group carried a flashlight and at least one spare. A few wore head lamps and helmets. Without light, a cave explorer would be lost down here. Only one person thought to bring knee pads—they would have been helpful.

It was cool down there, about forty-five degrees, but the exertion made the extra sweater unnecessary. Moisture on the ceiling sparkled in the light of headlamps and voices echoed off the rock cave walls, making it difficult to tell which direction they came from.

For most of the way, the tube varied from fifteen to twenty feet high, and from ten to fifteen feet across. We walked through vaults that rose to thirty-five feet and squeezed through claustrophobia-inducing crawl spaces little more than a couple of feet in diameter.

The rock was a dark gray, with some areas of reddish brown. But the color was hard to see in the feeble glow of flashlights.

As we neared the end, the cave began to shrink. Walking upright became impossible. Then, there was barely room to crawl. Finally the space narrowed to inches, making passage into the darkness beyond impossible.

We took a break to study the maps spread on the sandy floor. The cave's namesake lake marked on the map was nowhere to be found. The floor apparently had filled with sand since our map was drawn. This was as far as we could get.

After a short break, we started back toward the entrance—over, under and through all the same obstacles. But from the opposite direction it was hard to tell whether this was the pile of rocks we had climbed over, or the one we crawled under.

Then we reached the ladder. One by one, we climbed while others held it steady.

Soon, we could smell it. I felt a cool, sweet breath of air on my face. Then I could see light, green plants and the outside, sunlit world.

After a lunch break and a short drive, we hiked three-quarters of a mile through thick forest to a clearing and the yawning entrance of a second cave—Ole's Cave.

A spot where the cave ceiling had caved in—known as a skylight—formed the entrance and the way down over the tumbled rocks threatened twisted ankles. We entered the gloom again.

This lava tube is negotiable for about a mile and gains about three hundred feet of elevation along the way. Ole Peterson, a local farmer, discovered the cave in 1895.

He led tours, making it the first commercial cave in the state.

For much of its length, the cave averages about ten feet high and fifteen feet wide. But it narrows to a short passage maybe three feet in diameter—passable only on hands and knees on a hard knobby lava floor. This was one place where knee pads would have come in handy.

In several places, during its formation, small chunks of the ceiling had fallen onto the still-molten floor, leaving solidified concentric splash rings from eighteen inches to more than two feet across. About a quarter-mile from the entrance, a rock formation on the left wall resembles George Washington's profile.

Farther along, daylight pierced the gloom where other ceiling cave-ins have created skylights. The fourth such opening formed the exit. We clambered back out into the warm afternoon sun.

Cracks in the ground on the way back to the parked cars suggested other caves beneath our feet. The blasted summit of Mount St. Helens, visible through the trees, rose into a blue sky to the north.

A stop at the Cougar Bar and Grill for a bowl of homemade chili in the nearby town of Cougar gave us sustenance for the drive home. It was the best chili I ever tasted.

October 29, 2002

Giving thanks

The first piece of writing I ever got paid for was an essay on Thanksgiving, so I thought it appropriate to write something this week about the holiday.

Like most people in this country, I have a lot for which to be thankful.

I'm thankful for the opportunities to spend time outdoors—floating down a lazy river or hiking to the top of a mountain. And I'm thankful for the opportunity to get paid for writing about doing it.

I'm thankful that I had a house full of company again this year for a family-type celebration.

I guess my cooking didn't scare them off last year.

This year, I wised up and bought a fresh turkey so I wouldn't forget to thaw it. All I had to do was stuff it, shove it in the oven, open a beer and sit back for three or four hours.

I like Thanksgiving. This time of year means cold

nights, frost on the ground, migrating geese honking overhead. It means snow will soon be falling in the mountains. And it means that Christmas is just around the corner.

Changing seasons invigorate me. The paths I traced all summer are new. Most of the leaves are gone, many of them soften my step, and I can see farther into the woods.

The naked trees look like pencil drawings in the mist. The paths are muddier, and fewer people are out and about. There is a frosty bite to the early mornings, and the perfume-smell of burning alder hangs in the air.

Birds are coming into their winter plumage, and a variety of ducks and other water birds have returned to the waters around Puget Sound.

Recent rains have swelled some Western Washington rivers, and that is welcome news for salmon and other fish that now can complete their mating destiny and breathe a little easier.

But mostly I am amazed at the undaunted chum salmon. Despite all the pollution and sewage we dump into Puget Sound, they keep coming back—three million strong this year.

These fish and the incessant rain remind me of David James Duncan, one of the West's top fly-fishing writers, who suggests the quintessential Northwest Thanksgiving dinner should include salmon as an expression of thankfulness for the November rains that make the annual salmon runs possible.

I don't think he was stalking chum in the Oregon rivers of his youth, but I like his sentiment.

I love salmon, and the connection makes it a little

easier to put up with the long rainy spells in Washington. I just wonder, how cranberry sauce would taste with barbecued salmon or steelhead.

November 29, 2002

A writer's dilemma

It's a real dilemma. I write about great places to go and things to do outdoors.

Hey, sounds like fun, huh? It is, and I've seen a lot of beautiful country.

I know places where I can walk in any direction for hours without encountering another human. Places I can drive to, park the car and get out and the only sound is the beating of my own heart—or the sighing of the wind.

But like the angler who won't divulge the location of a favorite fishing hole, I am reluctant to say where those places are—for the same reasons.

I am reluctant to write about quiet places, where I can find solitude, peace.

Yet as an outdoor writer I often find myself writing about great places to go and things to do there. But I fear the attention I bring to these places would attract so many people that they would be ruined or so crowded they would no longer be worth visiting. Solitude is one thing you can't share.

Someone would be talking too loud on a cell phone, children yelling. People would leave their litter—disposable diapers, used condoms, empty beer cans, fishing lure packaging, old newspapers, fast-food wrappers.

People would trample the plants, break branches off the trees and scare off the wildlife. Not that anyone means any harm, but that simply comes from the crush of numbers.

How can I write about those places without ruining them?

Maybe the answer is just to write about places where lots of people go already. And a lot of those places are still worth going—if you can find a place to park. But if they're already overrun with outdoor enthusiasts, there's really no point in publicizing them.

So, just what is a fellow to do?

Maybe it's time to reflect on why I spend time outdoors. What's important is the experience of being out in nature, connecting with the landscape, no matter where that happens—on the beach, at a local city park or in the depths of a national park.

It doesn't matter where. It doesn't have to be in those places where lots of people like to go. I think there may be another answer.

An elderly gentleman, an avid hiker, told me not long ago, that most people won't go more than half a mile from their car. And after a couple of miles, you've weeded out most of the rest.

So, if I want a little peace and quiet, all I have to do

is hike a couple of miles farther into the woods. Granted that doesn't work everywhere. Some places are just so great that people go there even if they have to walk several miles—thousands of people hike up on Mount Rainier every summer.

And sometimes, just when you think you've put enough distance between yourself and the crowd, you get passed by a bunch of people on ATVs.

It's getting harder, but it's still possible to find places to get away. If they were easy to find they'd be overrun. Right?

I will look a little harder, walk a little farther or round just one more bend.

Why just the other day, I was driving down ...

December 13, 2002

Dreaming of Boats

Abandoned boat, Stanwood, Washington

In deep snow

One moment I was making my way between two young Douglas fir trees covered with snow like so many flocked Christmas trees—-the next moment I was eye-level with my own foot prints.

I was learning to snowshoe in deep snow on a forty-five degree slope near Stampede Pass, in the Cascade Mountains east of Seattle. The passage between the two trees was just too narrow for a pair of snowshoes.

And there I was, helpless, stuck in a tree well, barely able to move.

One snowshoe had come off; the other was tangled in the tree's lower branches. I struggled in vain. But a capable snowshoer pulled me to safety. I was lucky. People have died falling into and being stuck in a tree well—especially if you go in head first. Unhurt but wiser, I had learned an important outdoor lesson about heading out alone in places where stuff you don't know about can in fact hurt you, or worse.

In deep snow, many young evergreens shed snow around their perimeter, but only a little reaches the ground close to the trunk and under the branches. The result is a hole in the snow, wider at the top and partly obscured by branches. The depth of the hole depends on the snow pack. The one I went into was maybe five feet deep.

If you fall into one headfirst and you struggle to get out, the snow you knock down into the bottom can cover your head and suffocate you. It can be deadly.

On this winter Sunday, I had joined a class on winter travel and safety—Nordic skiing and snowshoeing safely in the back country on a weekend field trip to the Mountaineers' Meany Lodge at Stampede Pass, built in 1928. And we came out to get some exercise and have fun in the snow.

Just getting to Stampede Pass was an adventure. After following a fleet of snowplows across Snoqualmie Summit, I turned up the road to a Sno-Park parking lot. There a 1940s vintage Sno-Cat picked up passengers heading for the lodge. It was something out of a Humphrey Bogart movie. Above the distinctive Sno-Cat bulldozer tracks, narrow benches lined the steel deck, polished by many feet. The contraption was maybe twenty feet long and eight feet wide. A metal framework held up a plywood roof and a simple luggage rack. The sides had heavy rubberized tarps that kept out the cold only when the rig was not moving. Various boxes and racks fastened to the outside held skis, poles and other gear.

The driver in goggles and a scratched and dented helmet slipped into the cockpit-like driver's seat and grabbed the bulldozer controls. The African-Queenlooking contraption clanked, jolted and bounced its way along the snow-covered forest roads about three miles up to the lodge. Negotiating one hairpin turn required several tries.

The wind was free to rush from front to back once we started moving. The best seats were in the back, where warm air from the motor escaped. When the Sno-Cat was full—maybe thirty people—others would hitch a ride on skis or snowboards, towed by two ropes behind the cat.

Once at the lodge we all spilled out onto the snow. I strapped on a pair of rented snowshoes and set out with the class to get some practical experience. I learned not to fall into tree wells, and I learned how to climb steep hills by progressively kicking toeholds in the snow. Kick, step, rest—repeat. We moved slowly but steadily upward through the trees. This was easy. The trick was learning to keep my feet far enough apart than felt natural to avoid stepping on the other snowshoe, a move usually rewarded with an instant face plant—if you're lucky, in soft snow.

The trouble began when we started back down. The leader and instructor demonstrated by stepping off and sliding downhill about ten feet. The cleats on the snowshoes will stop you when you lean forward, he said, deftly demonstrating what looked like a simple maneuver.

Hah.

As novices, we weren't quite convinced. It took a little practice, and several falls—just to let go. Once you get sliding—an ungraceful glissade, really—in addition to maintaining your balance, you have to avoid small trees. I usually fell before I got to the leaning forward part. But the snow was forgiving that day, with about eight inches of fresh snow.

The Sunday outing ended with a ride in the fading daylight back down the same road with Bogart at the controls again. Riders tired from a day in the snow were less boisterous that on the way up.

I had some bruises and a sore leg from my encounter with the tree well, and I was glad when the behemoth snow-machine stopped in the parking lot. I had learned something more than just walking on snow. I learned about tree wells—something I didn't know existed before encountering one—and the importance of avoiding them.

If my friends hadn't pulled me out, I might still be up there, stuck under that young Douglas-fir, or at least until the snow melted.

January 21, 2003

Grab a map and go camping

Going camping? Times have changed. Boot up the computer.

Huh?

That's right!

It used to be that camping required a pair of good boots, rain gear, a tent and a camp stove. Now, it seems, the most important piece of gear is a computer and high-speed Internet access.

State and federal agencies now process reservations for campgrounds and wilderness camping on the Internet.

It's still possible to go camping without making a reservation. Many campgrounds still leave a few spots open to folks, who like me, are incapable of planning even a wienie roast, or who don't have a computer, and don't have reservations.

But increasingly, anyone who wants to camp at a

specific campground at a specific time needs to make a reservation—six months or more in advance at the most popular sites. Doing it on the Internet is more convenient for those with a home computer, and easier than doing it on the phone or in person.

The federal government's Internet reservation site warns that anyone who doesn't have a reservation might be doomed to wander in search of a place to pitch their tent or park their RV come summer. You can make a reservation up to 240 days in advance—a year for group sites.

The system is a partnership among the Forest Service, the Army Corps of Engineers and the Bureau of Land Management, which hired a company called ReserveAmerica, part of Ticketmaster, to run the reservation system.

ReserveAmerica couldn't tell me how much of my camping fee they get to keep. But in an e-mail exchange, ReserveAmerica Webhelp No. 4, known only as Eleonore, informed me: "All of the fees go to the Forest Service. They then credit our business for each of the transactions we perform for the customer. I am unable to provide you with exact dollar amounts."

The reservation system, however, listed a $9 reservation fee for an $8-per-night campsite at one of my favorite campgrounds on Baker Lake in northwest Washington. That's $17 for an $8 campsite—for the first night, after that it would be only $8 a night. But you lose your money if you don't show up.

State parks are cheaper. The Washington Parks and Rec's Internet system charges only $7 to make campground reservations.

I have a better idea.

Whatever happened to throwing the tent, sleeping bags and some grub in the back of the truck, lashing the canoe on top and heading into the woods? It's still possible to find a nice place off the road by a small lake or a nice stream, with the sweet smell of blooming cottonwoods in the breeze.

Best of all, it doesn't cost anything. Zip. Nada. And you don't need to own a computer or to know how to navigate the Internet. Let others struggle with usernames that haven't already been used and passwords at least eight characters long—and impossible to remember.

I'd rather lower my expectations and head for some out of the way spots. A good map, available for less than the campground reservation fee, will be useful for many adventures—my personal favorite is still the 7.5-degree USGS topo maps along with a standard state roadmap to get you into the general vicinity, and as much trouble as you can stand.

If you're looking for something a little more structured, most western states offer some free campsites. Some national forests charge for camping, but you don't need a reservation, and a few are free.

But for the truly adventurous—head for the end of the road and find a level spot not too far from a lake or river. Don't forget to bring your own drinking water, and that far up the creek, you better bring an extra paddle.

January 24, 2003

Singles' bars for crows

Crows will fly many miles to mingle with other crows. It's a social thing—mostly. They gather in nocturnal roosts in big trees with other birds, sometimes by the hundreds.

Like a downtown barroom on a Saturday night, singles on the make.

Early one winter day in the Nisqually Delta, about an hour south of Seattle, I passed a sixty-foot big-leaf maple full of crows, hundreds of them jostling each other for the best positions. None were in the other trees nearby—just in that particular tree. I have often seen such gatherings, but I made up my mind to call up an expert to find out why they do it.

"They are very social," John Marzluff told me. He is professor of wildlife science at the University of Washington and has a doctorate in zoology. He knows a lot about crows. Such group roosts are common in fall and winter, and crows will fly many miles to gather in nocturnal roosts with other birds.

They do it for a variety of reasons, Marzluff said. It's a good place for single crows to find mates. But that's not the only reason. In winter the birds are not mating or defending territory, and so they are more likely to gather with others. Parents, who are monogamous, may bring their young of that year to show off at the gathering. The gregarious birds find a common defense from great horned owls, red tail hawks and humans. The group shares good food sources, and the large number of birds generates a good deal of heat on a cold winter night.

And they come for social interaction.

Speaking of social interaction, crows also have one of the closest relationships with humans of any wild animal. Crows and humans have influenced each other over the centuries. They have influenced our culture with phrases and words, such as: to crow about something, crowbar, crow's nest; and our pop music with groups such as Counting Crows and Stone the Crows. Native mythology considered the crow a creator and trickster along with the raven—the crow's larger cousin. Human association of crows with darkness and evil may have its roots in the birds' carrion eating habits—habits that included human remains on battlefields. But crows don't slaughter their own kind.

Humans in turn have influenced crow behavior. Our own sloppy habits have created food sources previously unavailable to crows, including garbage dumps, road kill, uneaten French fries and other happy meal leftovers. They were quick to move into the Olympic Peninsula rainforest when humans opened large campgrounds in a place they wouldn't otherwise inhabit.

In his book, "In the Company of Crows and Ravens," Marzluff recounts a group of crows that returned year after year to a parking lot at the University of Washington that years ago had been a municipal garbage dump. Even after the dump was paved over the crows kept coming back each year—something they learned from their parents.

The birds are shiny black, eighteen to twenty inches long. They eat a lot of insect pests, but they also steal eggs from other birds, especially robins. They are patient with their young. Their scientific name, *Corvus brachyrhynchos*, means short billed corvid. Indeed a crow's bill is noticeably smaller than a raven's. Crows utter a variety of sounds, from the loud raucous "CAW" to a soft, purr-like rattle. They are intelligent, inquisitive and adaptable opportunists. They learn fast.

"They're hard to catch the second time," Marzluff said.

And that's not so different from my own experience on the singles scene in years past.

February 7, 2003

Dreaming of boats

Twice already in early 2003, my job took me to boat shows. It's sheer torture. The kind of boats on display are designed to make boat enthusiasts like me drool. Alas, the kind of boats I dream about are expensive—and I couldn't even afford to rent the slip at the marina.

That doesn't keep me from dreaming about buying one. I probably always will. But I'll probably never own one.

I already own a sixteen-foot canoe, but I'm talking about a sailboat you can spend a weekend on, perhaps with a couple of friends, or spend a week sailing in the San Juans or up the Inside Passage.

Sometimes the fantasy is just better than reality. You never have to paint or scrape barnacles off a fantasy, and they never tip over—er, capsize.

But talk to most boaters and they will tell you, there's something about being on the water.

Water Rat, in Kenneth Grahame's Wind in the Willows, said it best: "Believe me, my young friend, there is nothing—absolutely nothing—half so much worth doing as simply messing about in boats."

Being on the water just calms the nerves. It's soothing. After just a few minutes, the urgency of the work-a-day world dissolves. For me it usually takes about fifteen minutes.

While I put my canoe in the water, I'm still anxious about the things I ought to be doing. What if a wind comes up and I'm late for work; what if I tip the boat over; what if—hey, relax.

After a few minutes, my mind untangles, and my focus changes as I reconnect with the natural world. Perhaps it is because on the water I realize that I am no longer in complete control. I am at the mercy of the currents, tides and winds—things that require immediate attention.

I have been in enough bad weather and rough water to know. Back on land it is easier to pretend I am in control.

My wife gets nervous whenever we're around boats, and I get all moon eyed over some gracious vessel riding seductively on the water. I can't convince her that I'll probably go to my grave fantasizing about boats.

I can't help it. I'm Scandinavian. I'm genetically programmed to dream about owning a boat. In fact, I can't comprehend how a human being could be conscious and not love boats.

A local sailor was gracious enough to teach me a sheet from a shroud, a main from a jib and a jibe from a tack, and how to get the most out of the wind without tipping over.

But a boat can be a demanding mistress. I know enough about boats to know that you don't really own them—they own you. Not that the arrangement is necessarily unpleasant. Owning a boat would be so absorbing, I would probably willingly give up all my other hobbies.

I love my canoe, and I love the hours I spend in it. And maybe some summer I'll take a week to paddle up Ross Lake in the North Cascades, camping along the way.

For now I'm content to paddle up quiet streams and inlets and only dream about cruising open water in a sailboat, with the tiller in one hand, sheet in the other, the wind in my face, the quiet gurgle of water against the hull, the scenery, the snap of Dacron as wind fills the sail.

March 20, 2003

Leave the babies alone

Occasionally Mother Nature provides a marvelous a spectacle—sometimes subtle like the metallic iridescence of a hummingbird, sometimes overwhelming like the thousands of shorebirds that descend on Grays Harbor's Bowerman Basin on the Washington coast every spring.

Recently during a lunch break, I spied a fleet of red-breasted mergansers—forty-two of them—steaming purposefully, like an invading armada, from the east side to the west side of Budd Inlet. I was parked at the north end of the port peninsula in downtown Olympia, and watched the birds while eating my lunch.

Perhaps half a dozen of the birds were males in their full breeding plumage, with distinctive ragged crests that look like they forgot to comb their hair when they got up. The rest were not-so-flashy females with similar crests.

They dive for their food—small fish, aquatic insects and crustaceans.

What a great sight. I've never seen so many mergansers at once.

A curious harbor seal poked its head up to check out the fleet and startled a red-necked grebe also in breeding plumage, and feeding nearby.

Spring is a good time to watch birds and other wildlife. It's mating season for many species, and they are particularly active and visible. Many are too busy with, er, other things, to notice wildlife voyeurs quietly watching.

Almost half the state's population participates in watching wildlife. A 2001 U.S. Fish and Wildlife Service survey figured the number of participants at about 2.5 million. They're big business too. Wildlife watchers spent almost $1 billion on trips and equipment in 2001.

But leave the babies alone.

With all this breeding going on, baby critters will start popping up pretty soon. The whole point of this column— watch, but don't touch.

It's important, no matter how tempting, to leave the babies alone. It's important to keep a respectful distance—as I learned in a painful lesson from a great horned owl a few years ago.

I learned that if I encounter young, such as fawns seemingly abandoned, to leave them alone. Most likely their mothers are off feeding nearby and will return to suckle their young. Resist any temptation to help young animals that appear abandoned.

It's OK to check back in a few hours. It's natural for adults to leave their young alone for short periods.

Does often leave their fawns hunkered down in the brush while they forage nearby. Harbor seals often leave their pups on the beach as they hunt the waters offshore.

Baby seals are particularly vulnerable. They're not very smart and might mistake a well intentioned person for their mother and try to follow them. You should stay at least 150 feet away if you encounter one on the beach.

When the mother comes back, she may not be able to find the pup.

If they're still there after a few hours, contact wildlife officials or the local sheriff.

May 1, 2003

Arctic wildlife, oil, controversy

I t's a place I have always wanted to visit, to float down the wild Hulahula River north out of the Brooks Range to the Beaufort Sea, to camp on the fragile arctic plain that is home to vast herds of caribou, polar bears, wolves, musk ox and millions of birds.

Conservationists call it America's Serengeti.

Oil industry officials call it Area-1002.

The native Gwich'in people, who rely on the caribou that give birth in the area, call it "the place where life begins."

Regardless of what you call it, the 1.5-million-acre coastal plain of the Arctic National Wildlife Refuge—ANWR for short—is home to a long-running controversy as vast as the vistas from the flanks of the Sadlerochit Mountains.

To me it sounds like the ultimate outdoor adventure—the heart of wildness.

The area has been getting more attention locally for its outdoor recreation potential and controversial oil development. Oil industry officials, who want to develop the area's potential crude oil, say development and wildlife can coexist. The oil would mean new jobs and would reduce the country's dependence on oil imports— especially from Persian Gulf countries.

Conservationists want it left alone, undeveloped, saying the amount of oil likely to be found would make little difference. And the Gwich'in say development would mean the end to their way of life.

I don't want to take sides, but some time ago I had a chance to speak with an oil expert.

"Nobody knows how much oil there is in ANWR," said Ken Boyd, geophysicist and oil industry consultant. Seismic and other evidence says there is some oil there. Estimates vary greatly: Geologists say there is a ninety-five-percent chance of finding sixteen billion barrels and a five-percent chance of finding up to forty-two billion barrels. The amount that can be economically recovered depends on technology and the price of oil.

Conservationists cite an earlier U.S. Geological Survey estimate of 3.6 billion barrels. Boyd's middle-of-the-road estimate is ten billion barrels of recoverable oil. A barrel is forty-two gallons.

"But nobody knows until you drill," he said. And for that, the oil companies need the approval of Congress.

Regardless of how much oil is found, it would come through the Trans-Alaska Pipeline System, which has a maximum capacity of just over two million barrels per day. It has been pumping about one million barrels per day—enough to meet about five percent of the country's daily consumption, which is roughly twenty million barrels per day, or about seven billion barrels per year.

The United States imports about fifty-eight percent, or a little more than eleven million barrels, of the daily consumption. Most of that comes from Canada, Venezuela, Mexico and other countries. About 2.6 million barrels per day—or about thirteen percent—comes from Persian Gulf countries. So unless another pipeline is built, the oil found beneath the wildlife refuge could not replace all the oil imported from the Persian Gulf.

Meanwhile, 130,000 caribou of the Porcupine herd migrate to the coastal plain to give birth to their young in most years. The Gwich'in people fear oil development would interrupt the cycle of caribou migration and birthing on the coastal plain. The animals sometimes wade into the ocean to escape the swarms of mosquitoes. To get there, they would have to run a gantlet of haul roads and pipelines, noisy diesel trucks and heavy equipment, drilling rigs, helicopters and perhaps bored, off-duty oil field workers with high powered rifles.

I'd still like to see the area before it's developed—even with the dense swarms of Alaskan mosquitoes. I wonder how oil development would affect recreation. Would canoe trips down wild rivers go the way of the caribou? I wonder what people would say about oil rigs in Kenya's Masai Mara, or Yellowstone's Lamar Valley.

May 15, 2003

Cougar encounter

I haven't seen one since I was a child, but I'm sure I've been watched by more than one while hiking and camping.

About three weeks ago, on May 8, a Fort Lewis man who had a twenty-five-pound Chinook salmon strapped to his back met a cougar with a taste for fish. The man, who didn't want his name made public, had the salmon wrapped in plastic and strapped to his backpack when the cougar knocked him down near the Kalama River.

The man, in his mid-thirties, had spent the morning fishing the Kalama River, about thirty miles north of Portland, Oregon. He was hiking out with his catch just before 11 a.m. when he was knocked down from behind. As he rolled on his side to get up, he saw what he described as a huge cougar disappearing into the brush twelve to fifteen feet away.

The startled angler wasn't injured, but the backpack

showed claw marks. He hiked out to a nearby store to reported the incident.

The Washington Department of Fish and Wildlife brought in a private hound hunter who searched the area about ten miles northeast of Kalama for several hours. Hounds picked up the cougar's scent, but they didn't find the cat before dark.

Officials considered the incident serious. Under state policy, cougars that attack humans are tracked and killed.

Cougars seem to inspire awe and fear out of proportion to their actual toll on humans.

In the past one hundred years, fewer that twenty people have been killed and about seventy-five people have been injured by cougars in North America.

In that same time, more than fifteen thousand people have been killed by lightning; ten thousand by collisions with deer; four thousand by bees; and thirteen hundred by rattlesnake bites.

Of the twelve cougar attacks in Washington, ten occurred during the 1990s. Not all of those qualify as physical attacks on humans. But the Washington Department of Fish and Wildlife considers any incident where a cougar makes contact with a human as an attack. No contact, no attack.

The only fatality was a thirteen-year-old child in 1924 in Okanogan County in eastern Washington.

Meanwhile, humans killed three hundred cougars in Washington in 2001-2002—sixty-four of those out of concern for human safety.

An adult cougar can reach a length of nearly five feet with a three-foot tail. Adult males weigh up to two hundred pounds, and adult females up to one hundred twenty. They are able to leap twenty feet straight up and cover thirty feet on the level. They also are capable of short bursts of speed, but rely mostly on stealth to hunt.

They are known variously as cougar, mountain lion, catamount, puma and a few other things. Whatever you call them they are superb hunters—-the most successful and wide-spread carnivore in North America, found from Canada to Argentina, from sea level to fourteen thousand feet, from arctic tundra to tropical jungle.

Cougars are found throughout most of the Pacific Northwest. Like any other predator, the cougar population has grown in response to the growth of the deer population—their primary prey.

Urban development has encroached on the traditional deer habitat, and deer have sought refuge from hunters in those new subdivisions in the so-called urban-wildland interface. Cougars simply followed the prey into more populated areas, increasing the odds of interaction with humans.

Most cougar encounters go unnoticed by humans. But a few people do encounter cougars, either by chance or by stumbling upon a recent kill or a litter of kittens.

If a cougar is aggressive, the experts say the best course is to keep your eye on the cat, talk to it and back away slowly. Don't block its escape route. Pick up small children. Don't run. Face the cougar, raise your arms, spread your jacket to make yourself look as big as possible.

If the cat attacks, the experts say, fight back. Try to stay on your feet, throw rocks, hit it with a stick, a backpack, clothing or your bare hands it that's all you have. Make the cat realize you're a threat.

But all of that is easy to say, sitting here in my nice, comfortable office. It's another matter when you're sweating, your heart racing, and the cougar is staring at you from less than thirty feet away, ears back, teeth bared.

Or when you've just lost a nice salmon, ripped right off your back.

May 29, 2003

Trash is a no-brainer

Leaving trash is not unique to any particular group, age or sex. I see it everywhere people go outdoors. Pick it up, and pack it out.

Did your mother used to nag you to pick up your trash? Well, mine did. So, now I always keep a plastic garbage sack in the bag I carry on hikes or in my canoe. When I can, I pick up trash I find along the way—stuff that others have left, thinking no doubt that their mothers would be along soon to clean up after them. Or perhaps not thinking at all.

I find it floating in the water, at the put-in or along the trail—empty beer cans, discarded fishing tackle or the plastic wrapper it came in, the white plastic foam cups that night crawlers come in, spent shotgun shells, fast-food and energy-bar wrappers, disposable diapers, used condoms and all sorts of other yucky junk. Heck, one could spend all day just picking up stuff—I use a stick for some things.

Some fish and wildlife officials encourage all outdoor enthusiasts to make trash pickup a part of their outdoor routine. It's a good thing to do, and it demonstrates a person's commitment to conservation, they say.

I couldn't agree more.

It not only helps keep areas clean, but it builds family traditions. Children learn from their parents. If parents pick up their litter, their children learn to be good stewards of the land. If parents leave their litter all over, their children learn to be slobs, too. Picking up trash sets a good example.

Trash is everywhere along roads, trails, in campgrounds, parking areas and pullouts. But some people work harder at making a mess than others. None compares to the bullet-riddled refrigerators and shot-up washing machines, the shattered bottles and other cast-off household junk blasted beyond recognition at makeshift shooting ranges. One of the reasons some private lands are closed to public access is that too many irresponsible people dump their trash—holed and otherwise—along the roads.

Not everyone who plays outdoors is a slob. In fact, a lot of outdoor people are pretty good about not leaving their trash around, but it only takes one or two slobs to ruin what was a nice place to fish, camp or put a canoe in the water.

I feel a sense of responsibility to keep the places I use clean. I mean, nobody likes to camp and hike or picnic in a garbage dump.

Besides being unsightly, litter presents a threat to wildlife. Birds get tangled and injured or killed by abandoned fishing tackle; small mammals get stuck in plastic six-pack holders. Skunks have been known to die after getting their heads stuck in some kinds of yogurt cups.

A good way to avoid leaving trash behind is to plan ahead—bring a garbage sack and use it. And pack things that are easy to bring home. It is one way to be considerate of the people and other creatures with whom we share the woods and waters. It takes only a moment to inspect a campsite for trash and pick it up. If we carry the stuff in, what's so hard about carrying the empties back out?

Seems like a no-brainer.

June 15, 2003

Passion becomes a career

I first ran into him on a sunny summer afternoon in the Quinault rainforest in Washington's Olympic National Forest, where he led guided walks as a seasonal ranger with the U.S. Forest Service.

Then one day last winter, I happened to stop at the Nisqually Reach Nature Center, and there he was inside with answers to my questions about the expansive delta where the Nisqually River runs into southern Puget Sound.

And if you visit the U.S. Fish and Wildlife Service's Nisqually National Wildlife Refuge during the weekend you're likely to run into him there as well.

This guy gets around.

Daniel Hull, 34, lanky, with long reddish hair works for the Nature Center, and he's a part-time ranger at the refuge. Hull is knowledgeable, engaging and enthusiastic. When I encountered him, he gave a clear presentation, explaining in simple terms the complex interconnections among the plants and animals in the coastal old-growth forest.

I marveled at delicate muscles rippling along the belly of a large brown forest slug when he held it upside down. That's how it moves, he said.

He obviously has a passion for the outdoors and nature, and he obviously likes sharing his passion.

I ran into Hull again the other day—rather I sought him out. We spent some time at the Nature Center overlooking the Nisqually mud flats alive with birds. We talked as we watched eagles, herons, gulls, crows, swallows and purple martins, with the bulk of Mount Rainier rising in the distance into a clear blue summer sky.

As the caretaker and coordinator of activities at the Nisqually Reach Nature Center, Hull is the first paid employee of the nonprofit organization. He lives in the building, but he didn't take the job for the money.

"I live in the most beautiful place," Hull said with a sweeping gesture in the direction of Mount Rainier rising in the distance above the mud flats of the Nisqually Delta. "I have no gripes."

On that particular day, I would have to agree. The sun and the tide both were out. The inspiration for his outdoor career came during a hike up the Enchanted Valley in the Olympic National Park. After high school he and some friends had traveled around the country, visiting as many national parks and forests as they could before heading off to college.

In the park, they ran into a ranger who went out of his way to be helpful and informative. Hull was impressed and decided he'd like a job like that. He went back home to Ohio and finished a degree in natural science.

Upon graduation he got a seasonal job with the U.S. Forest Service at the Mount St. Helens National Volcanic Monument. It was his chance to work outdoors. That was thirteen years ago. He's still here, and he's still working outdoors.

From Mount St. Helens he went to work at Quinault, where he spent nine years, and where during one winter storm it rained as hard as it can rain for 36 hours without letup. Even that didn't dampen his enthusiasm.

"I still deeply love the Quinault," he said.

For Hull it's a spiritual thing. He feels a deep connection with nature. And he has a sense of mission. People live in cities and spend their days in front of a computer, he said. But in their off hours, they flock to parks and forests, trying to reconnect with nature. Part of his job has been to help them make that connection, he said.

He tries to convey a message to people by raising questions, not to get a particular answer, but to get people to think, and he shares what he thinks is important. Hull hopes to instill an environmental ethic—one person at a time.

He still thinks of himself as just an ordinary guy. He's anything but.

June 22, 2003

Bureaucracy swamps safety

In the wake of a charter boat tragedy at Tillamook Bay on the Oregon coast in the summer of 2003, the question of marine safety and who enforces which rules came up.

So I thought I would include some basic safety information in a story I was working on that summer about the opening of the salmon season off the west coast of Washington.

On the morning of June 14, the Taki-Tooo swamped while trying to cross the ocean bar at the mouth of Tillamook Bay, against the tide on a stormy day. Despite small craft warnings along the coast and rough bar warning at the Tillamook Inlet, the charter boat headed out into ten-foot swells for a day of fishing in the ocean.

The boat capsized and ten passengers and the captain died. The remaining seven passengers and the single deckhand survived with minor injuries. Despite Coast

Guard regulations for rough water, the captain had not required the passengers to wear life jackets.

To learn more about such regulations, I started, full of hope, by calling the Coast Guard station in Westport. It seemed the logical place to start.

Alas, I ran aground on the shoals of government bureaucracy.

A cheerful petty officer in Westport told me that marine safety questions must be deferred to the Seattle or Portland MSO—marine safety office. He gave me the number for the Portland office, where I was transferred to a businesslike lieutenant.

She asked me to submit my questions in an e-mail because the office had been getting so many requests for similar information since the Taki-Tooo went down.

I sent off my e-mail on a Monday.

I asked simple questions about the basic safety requirements for charter boats. Are life jackets required? Life rafts? Are boats inspected? How often? By whom? What can passengers on charter boats do to protect themselves?

The lieutenant told me to call her back if I hadn't gotten a response to my questions by the end of the next day. That was Tuesday. No one responded.

Wednesday morning the lieutenant confessed she had lost my phone number. She would have called to tell me, but because of the volume of media interest in marine safety, all calls were now being handled by the Seattle marine safety office.

She gave me the Seattle number. A petty officer in Seattle listened carefully to my request, and then he said the office had been getting so many requests for similar information that I would have to submit my questions in an e-mail.

I suggested he call the woman in the Portland office and have her forward the e-mail I already had submitted. He thought that was a good idea—someone would get back to me with answers to my questions by the end of the day.

No one did.

Thursday morning another energy-efficient petty officer in the Seattle office told me I had to talk to vessel licensing and documentation. OK, can you transfer me?

After few minutes on hold, she said that because of the ongoing investigation into the capsizing of the Taki-Tooo she could not comment on anything regarding charter boat safety.

Are charter boats required to carry life jackets?

"I don't have that information, sir," she said defensively.

Surely there are written rules somewhere detailing the basic requirements?

"I don't have that information, sir," she repeated, obviously running out of patience.

The rules, it turns out, are available online in 46 CFR, subchapter T. Those rules say the captain must make passengers wear life jackets during hazardous conditions—such as crossing the Tillamook bar during bad weather. The captain of Taki-Tooo gave passengers a safety briefing, but he did not require them to wear life jackets.

Waves at the mouth of the bay were eight to ten feet, and a small craft warning was in effect—a small craft is anything thirty-three feet long and under. The Taki-Tooo—thirty-two and a half feet long—was capsized by a fifteen-foot wave.

The Westport Charterboat Association, in Westport, Washington, understandably sensitive, always takes safety seriously.

The charter boats I've been aboard have conducted safety briefings before leaving the dock. They have explained important safety features, like the location of the head and the coffee pot, where to find life jackets and life rafts and emergency procedures.

Still, going out over the bar—that shallow area of choppy water where river meets ocean waves—can be a little hair-raising, and passengers may be asked to stay seated through the rough water.

Whenever it's rough, the Coast Guard requires passengers wear life jackets while going out over the bar, the charter boat association executive director told me.

That doesn't seem too hard. Why couldn't the Coast Guard just tell me that?

For me personally, however, if it's going to be so rough that I need a life jacket, I'd just as soon stay ashore.

June 29, 2003

Experience the great indoors

The outdoors has been captured and is being held captive in four giant buildings somewhere in the Midwest.

A company that owns a series of theme parks is touting northwoods-themed indoor resorts, saying the parks are revolutionizing family vacations.

The company says it offers a high-quality resort vacation experience for families year round.

"Families are virtually guaranteed a fun, successful vacation," says the Great Lodge Family of Resorts Web site. You can challenge your family members to a game of Parcheesi in front of a stone fireplace with a family of stuffed wolves looking on with unseeing glass eyes.

Here you can find excitement and comfort and family-size suites; indoor water parks and outdoor recreation areas; casual, themed restaurants; theaters and an arcade, all under a climate-controlled roof.

You think I'm kidding? There's more.

There are water slides, pools, a fake river, whirlpools and wading pools safe for even the youngest adventure seeker—all with bathtub warm water. For the children there are activity rooms, with arts, crafts and educational programs.

They offer manicured, safe outdoor-themed fun—story time by the fireplace. A mechanical moose sings to the children. For the grown-ups there are facials, massages, pedicures, manicures and a hair salon.

Flush toilets and hot showers.

No more driving for hours, trying to find a camping spot, or struggling to put up the tent in the dark, only to discover that you forgot fuel for the camp stove.

No catholes here. No breathtaking, ice-cold mountain streams. No eau de skunk. No steep trail to hike to stunning vistas. No poison ivy to avoid. No rattlesnakes or xexenes.

The Great Lakes Companies Inc. says it is trying to provide themed year-round resorts—primarily indoor water parks—not to replicate the outdoors in an indoor setting.

Good. Because anything else would be pretentious and downright dishonest.

"Outdoor-themed" anything is no substitute for the real thing. To me the point of the outdoors is to interact with nature, to know hot, cold, rain, snow, sun, birds, rattlesnakes, cougars and bears. To say nothing of tired feet and aching muscles.

Themed resorts can teach visitors a lot about animals and their habitat. So can the Discovery Channel. I wonder how much habitat was wiped out and paved over to build these resorts.

But to me, the outdoors teaches far more. I have learned to evaluate and manage risks and to set up a tent in the dark when it's windy and raining. I have learned to make fire with a couple of sticks and a piece of string. I have learned that fresh bear poop on the trail means being alert and careful where I walk.

I have experienced the sublime, the sparkling of the dawn on a spider web, the gentle sigh or moan of the wind in tall firs; a mother moose and calf, feeding in the willows a few yards from my tent, and the earth-shaking power of storm-driven waves breaking on a Pacific Ocean beach.

How do you replicate the scent of pines on a hot day or the pungent perfume of sagebrush or rain-wet prairie grasses or the satisfaction of relaxing in a remote campsite after a strenuous hike?

More and more people seem to be trying to reconnect with nature—but you can't have the real thing without some risks and occasional discomforts.

It would be sad indeed, if themed resorts were the only way left to learn about nature. I don't have anything against them. But personally, I prefer my outdoors raw—not canned or predigested.

July 6, 2003

Savor the moments

That musical trilling—a red-winged blackbird. A haunting, lyrical upward spiraling song—the Swainson's thrush. A melodic phrase—either a song sparrow or a Bewick's wren. The high-pitched buzzing—a kinglet.

Any birder will tell you that a decent pair of binoculars and a good birding guide is all it takes to get started in learning to identify the local wild birds.

But I maintain you don't even need that. First, just stop and listen. I'm always pleasantly surprised at what I can hear in the woods when I stop walking and start listening.

I can hear them, but at first I can't see them. After I stop, I see movement. Something is flitting among the branches. It's a pair of Bewick's wrens. I begin to see more. On the ground on the other side of the trail a pair of spotted towhees are scratching in the leaves.

Deep in the woods, I can hear the spooky, plaintive tone of a varied thrush.

So much of what passes for outdoor recreation today is just an extension of the spend-more-money, hurry-up lifestyle we seem to be caught up in. But money is no substitute for time when it comes to relaxing a little and letting go of the stress.

For me a big part of outdoor recreation is relaxing and recharging my spiritual batteries. The whole point of taking time off from work is to not be in a hurry.

Stopping on a footbridge, I caught sight of a chestnut Virginia rail crossing the narrow creek. While I was stopped I heard the sound of a pair of song sparrows— one nearby and the other answering from deeper in the woods.

In the willow thickets of a wetland along the trail, I spotted an American goldfinch. In the trees on the other side of the trail I saw a yellow warbler—or perhaps it was a Wilson's warbler. And that was just one afternoon.

Sometimes birders disagree on the identification of a glimpsed bird. But even when the bird books come out, a positive identification is not always possible.

We reduce the identification to a number of probables. The process of elimination includes typical range, breeding plumage, feeding patterns, size and voice. Ultimately it doesn't matter what kind of bird it was. But in the process of trying to find out, I often learn something about the birds I think it may have been. I learn a little about their habitat and their habits, and a little bit about their lives.

The process sharpens the eye, and the powers of observation.

What about those prints in the mud. I wonder who might have walked here. Maybe a raccoon, or was it a muskrat or perhaps a beaver?

A pile of dark brown pellets and the imprint of a cloven hoof show a black-tailed deer passed here recently— probably earlier that day. The dung is fresh, and the hoof prints are sharply outlined in the soft dirt.

I breathe deeply of the forest perfume, sweet air cleaned and scented by the trees and undergrowth— buffered from the noise and stink of traffic.

The best part of all is I don't have to leave town to experience all these things. All I have to do is slow down, stop for a bit, exhale and just listen.

July 13, 2003

Part Two: Idaho

Warm Lake, Idaho

Blazing a new trail

In August 1988, I loaded my meager possessions into a U-Haul truck and left my temporary home in Tumwater, Washington. My car had conveniently died the day after I got the call from the newspaper in Twin Falls, Idaho, offering me a job.

It was hot, really hot, when I stopped for gas in Hermiston, Oregon, on my way to southern Idaho. I asked a guy in boots and blue jeans at the gas station how hot it was. "110, just right," he quipped. And it was but a taste of what I was heading into. The truck had no air conditioning, and the wind blew hot through the open windows of the cab. The heat did not relent despite the increasing altitude as I neared Twin Falls, where I spent my first night in a motel. After my first day at work I began looking for a place to rent and a car. It was the start of a new life for me.

I inherited restlessness and an appreciation for nature from my father. I remember fondly countless trips to Banff in the Canadian Rockies during the three years we lived in Calgary, Alberta. I remember on one trip we watched a deer drinking from the Bow River, when in a cougar-tawny flash the deer was gone.

But we moved a lot while I was growing up. By the time I graduated from high school, I had gone to ten schools in three countries. The wanderlust didn't end when I left home. After serving in the U.S. Navy during the Vietnam War, I worked for a few months in electronics in San Jose, California. I spent a summer in the Selkirk Mountains of eastern British Columbia. I hitch-hiked from Vancouver to Guatemala, where border officials turned me back. The trip back to California was full of magic moments, Entero-Vioformo and roadside romance. I returned to San Jose with $5 to my name.

A friend introduced me to semi-professional theatre. It was promising—I loved the intensity and creative atmosphere. But full-time, paying jobs in theatre were nearly impossible to find. I moved to Washington, where I fell in with a group of musicians and worked with a country-rock road band for a few years. In between I worked at a number of odd jobs—from pumping gas in a small town north of Seattle, to driving a cotton combine sixteen hours a day one central California winter.

Along the way, notions of writing began to take shape.

I wound up in a rented house at the edge of the woods outside Stanwood, Washington, where I pecked away at an old Royal manual typewriter in my time off. Then a friend suggested that if I wanted to be a writer, I should become a journalist—that way I could make a living and be a writer. I wouldn't have to write in my spare time. Great idea! Where do I start?

I started by enrolling at Western Washington University, which had one of the best journalism programs in the Pacific Northwest. While attending classes in Bellingham, I spent a lot of weekends in the wilds of the North Cascades, where I learned about old-growth forests, spotted owls before they were listed as an endangered species, wilderness and sleeping on the ground. I got a part-time work-study job with the Washington Department of Wildlife as a field research assistant, which amounted to about twenty hours a week with a notebook and binoculars tromping around in the Skagit River delta observing raptors. The research was part of the study that led to a ban on lead shot in waterfowl hunting. It rekindled my interest in nature and sharpened my taste for natural resource and environmental issues. I went on to complete bachelors degrees in journalism and environmental studies.

Shortly after I graduated, I applied for a job at the newspaper in Twin Falls. I knew nothing of the place when I went there to interview in late spring 1988. I would stay there until May 2001. During those years I would write about radioactive wastes in the Idaho desert, public land grazing, water rights and water fights, and many other public lands, natural resource and environmental issues. One of the things that kept in Twin Falls for all those years was the easy access to the outdoors, and the kinds of activities I enjoy. About forty minutes away to the south a four thousand-foot rise, known as the South Hills, offered hiking trails that turned to cross-country ski trails in the winter. Back roads that invited exploration stretched for unpaved miles into north-eastern Nevada and northwestern Utah. Endless vistas stretched to the horizon, unbroken by power poles or pavement. Dirt tracks traced rugged canyons, skirted lush beaver pond meadows, crossed sagebrush grasslands and threaded lodgepole and subalpine fir woods. Trails laced these hills, beckoning with day-long, over-night or longer hikes in varied terrain, some easy and some difficult. Wildlife here included mule deer, elk, California bighorn sheep, cougar and rumors of bears. One day I saw a golden eagle rise from the roadside with a jackrabbit in its talons. The hills were alive with songbirds and a variety of hawks and falcons—one day I spied a rare northern goshawk.

When the heat in the valley grew unbearable, it was always ten to twenty degrees cooler up here. One day while picnicking on a hilltop, I watched a small puff of cloud grow into thunderstorm with pounding rain that drove me to drier ground in the valley below.

A three hour drive north from Twin Falls took me into the scenic Sawtooth National Recreation Area with stunning scenery and bucolic views of the Sawtooth Valley. Cradling the headwaters of the storied Salmon River, the rugged Boulder-White Cloud Mountains lined the east side of the valley, and the even more rugged Sawtooth Mountain lined the west along with the Sawtooth Wilderness and numerous canoe-able lakes.

Closer to home, at the north edge of town the Snake River canyon dropped five hundred feet to a calm stretch of river, just perfect for a little paddling—it was close enough that I could be on the water within twenty minutes from my house. I spent many mornings on the river on days when I didn't have to be to work until noon.

Over the years, I spent countless hours paddling that

stretch of river, observing the wildlife, the deer that came down to drink, the beaver and muskrat that made a living in these quiet waters. Porcupines peered from trees, a colony of swallows built mud nests on the cliffs that rose straight out of the river, and twice I saw the pug marks of a cougar in the soft mud at the river's edge. Hawks and eagles soared on canyon rim thermals five hundred feet above my head, while kingfishers and great blue herons kept watch on the river.

In the early 1990s, I shared my exploits on the Snake River with the outdoor editor at the paper. He suggested I write up some of those adventures into occasional columns for the paper's weekly outdoors page. After few clumsy efforts, the column became more regular. Recognizing my reflective bent, the editor, an avid white-water canoeist, dubbed it "Quiet Waters."

A few of those early columns are included in the following pages.

Quiet Waters

Snake River Canyon, Twin Falls, Idaho

A morning's reflection

I t's not necessary to drive for hours, or face a grueling hike on steep trails to enjoy a little wildness. It's right here, on the very edge of town.

A half-hour after deciding to go, I can have my canoe gently bobbing in the water at the boat ramp at Centennial Park, in the Snake River Canyon just north of Twin Falls, in southern Idaho. In a few minutes I'm paddling upstream beneath the I.B. Perrine Memorial Bridge.

Down here, nearly five hundred feet below the canyon rim, it is peaceful on a September morning. A light breeze breaks up the reflection of the graceful arch of steel girders high above the water, and it pushes me gently upstream. My long-haired black, furry-faced friend samples the air for interesting scents.

Far across the pea-soup colored river a big fish jumps, and in the cattails near the shore something unseen rustles.

I like slipping quietly up on the wildlife—a deer

looks up from its drink, watches me watch it and goes unconcerned back to browsing. A small brown bat hovers a fraction of an inch above the water—just low enough to dip its tiny pink tongue into the river for a drink.

Above the rugged canyon rim, three turkey vultures make lazy circles in the deep blue sky. Above the opposite rim, several small birds haze a red-tailed hawk, which does its best to maintain its dignity—despite the harassment.

A muskrat looks up from sunning on the mud bank in an opening among the reeds. For a moment it looks like it's thinking about scurrying for cover, but it decides that I'm no threat and relaxes. Gnarled willow trees lean precariously out over the water, their lower limbs marking the surface in the gentle current.

Up near the canyon rim, thready, wind-blown waterfalls leap from the rocks only to dash themselves on moss covered rocks far below. The early morning sunshine sparkles on the falling water and lights up swarms of late-season insects.

In stark contrast to the wildness down along the river, traffic rumbles 480 feet above my head. Semi-trucks make the steel girders screech—unnerving in this flimsy craft below the bridge.

But down here the scene is stunning. In the low morning sun, the dry grasses on the canyon side look like velvet and dark basalt stands out in relief.

This beautiful piece of river is one of the best things about living in Twin Falls. It offers respite from the rat-race and a chance to connect with the natural systems that make our own lives possible.

The canyon slices through a layer cake of geologic

history, where years counted by the thousands are stacked in tiers of basalt on top of older rhyolite lava. The evidence of past changes are wedged between the basalt layers, sediments hardened by time and tortured rock fragments cemented together by sand and pressure.

Cracks in the brittle basalt and holes in the interstices form homes for hawks and pigeons, pack rats and other small creatures.

The changing seasons bring a variety of life and activities along the river. In late summer, beaver and muskrats are busy stocking succulent branches for leaner times ahead; yearling fawns are nearly grown, fat and sleek from summer's feeding

The swallows have raised their young and have long since abandoned their mud nests slung under overhanging rocks like so many Anasazi ruins. The young hawks have fledged and learned to work the strong canyon updrafts.

At the water's edge stands a great blue heron. Meditative, catatonic, the Zen master of the canyon, its lightning beak poised. With a prehistoric shriek, it lifts in ungainly flight.

But now the wind that pushed my craft gently upstream has grown strong, raising small whitecaps in the middle of the river. Getting home will be hard.

Working the wind, waiting for the gusts to subside, seeking the lee of shoreline points, I keep boat pointed into the largest waves. The rising wind turns a contemplative morning outing into a challenge.

But that, too, is the natural way of things.

September 21, 1995

Rim with a view

The day dawned clear, but it was too windy for a planned canoe trip on the river. So instead I pulled on my hiking boots and set off along the wild north rim of the Snake River Canyon, some five hundred feet above the second largest river in the West.

Up here it is possible to walk east along the canyon rim nearly ten miles with a couple of detours. I crossed the river on the Perrine Bridge and the highway heading north out of Twin Falls, Idaho, and turned onto a dirt road just across the river. I parked in the dusty weeds at the side of the road, laced up my boots and headed east.

The land here is heavily used by recreationists, livestock and wildlife. The dominant plants—rabbit brush, tansy mustard, snake weed, cheat grass, Russian thistle—are common on land that's been overgrazed or otherwise abused. But on this October morning, the tawny grasses, dusty green and yellow rabbit brush and tiny purple flowers dress up the dark basaltic rimrock.

A red fox has marked the narrow trails with scat, and marmots have left evidence scattered on a bare rock. A flock of crows bucked the wind and veered noisily across the river, like a gang of laborers heading off on a coffee break.

I have to watch my step near the rim. The footing is uncertain and a single misstep could result in a long tumble—straight down. I keep back from the edge, but I can't resist an occasional peek over the rim.

Far below, the sun sparkles off wind-driven ripples on the pea-green river. Through binoculars, I can make out the crumbling foundations of a house on a wide section of river bank. A rusting, horse-drawn sickle-bar mower sits in a field gone wild. The abandoned farmstead is isolated between the vertical canyon walls and the river.

Someone lived down there once, and for a time wrested a living from the long sliver of sandy soil—maybe a hundred yards at its widest. A rusting bedstead lies twisted in the weeds, along with a bottomless wash basin, parts of a wood-burning cook stove and other evidence of vanished dreams.

From the grassy river bank, a marsh hawk rises on the wind. With dihedral wings outstretched, the hawk—the only species of harrier found in North America—reaches a talon up to scratch its head. It turns and disappears upstream.

Though I try to stay close to the rim, loose footing makes me veer to the inside of a ridge of lava rock. Moments later, I arrive in an open bowl formed by a series of low lava ridges on three sides. At the bottom of the bowl is a maze of trails and burrows. It is the home of a family of red foxes. But the inhabitants are gone now, leaving only the wind's silken rustle.

Foxes normally use their dens only during spring and summer while they raise their young; during the rest of the year they rely on their speed and cunning. I saw the female here last spring and much of the evidence of her hunting remains—bones of small animals, and portions of animals too large to drag whole to her hungry pups.

The evidence of human activity is abundant as well— broken glass, beer cans, plastic bottles, spent shotgun shells and shattered clay pigeons. Perforated household appliances and assorted auto parts have been sacrificed for target practice.

Suddenly, a couple of aerial denizens rise into view just a few feet away, as an adult red-tail hawk followed closely by a juvenile ride an updraft like an elevator. They circle and glide barely moving their wings—most of the work is done by the tail—as the breeze lifts them and carries them along the canyon rim.

Swinging my gaze over the grassland, my binoculars easily pick out the dark belly band and white rump of a rough-legged hawk, hovering over unseen prey. This perennial winter resident has returned. The medium sized hawk spends its summer in the far north and winters here in southern Idaho. I wonder if its arrival so early portends an early winter.

It circles higher and higher on the wind then folds its wings and noses over into a steep dive. It spreads its wings again and flares its tail and floats to stall, before continuing its dive. It disappears behind a ridge after unseen prey. But it comes back up with nothing to show in its talons.

I made only a couple of miles this day, but I had not destination other than to be there. Along the dusty road home, a small flock of house finches feeds nervously on the dry heads of wild sunflowers. The rib cage of a mule deer fawn lies bleaching in the sun.

The wind whispers in my ear.

Nature has countless stories to tell here along the canyon rim for anyone willing to stop and listen.

October 12, 1995

Hidden retreat

L ike a Shangri-La hidden in a forbidden landscape, a bit of paradise lies hidden in the heart of Devils Corral, on the Snake River in southern Idaho.

From the boat ramp above Shoshone Falls, it's about a mile and a half by canoe to the foot of a thirty-foot waterfall tumbling over large rocks. The gin-clear creek belies the violent waters that fifteen thousand years ago carved out the multi-tiered labyrinth of alcoves, dry falls and plunge pools now known as Devils Corral.

The place, once a hide-out for nineteenth century horse thieves, is now a haven for wildlife and a popular recreational site—and it is well known to most people who grew up in this part of southern Idaho. But its mystique still provides the excitement of discovery to those who see it for the first time.

Etched into the north side of the Snake River Canyon, Devils Corral is hard, bony country. The topsoil here was washed away and area scoured down to bare basalt by the tremendous flood that drained ancient Lake Bonneville thousands of years ago.

More than 380 cubic miles of water rushed down the Snake River. At peak flows, water surged at fifteen million cubic feet per second—nearly seven billion gallons per second or one-third of a cubic mile of water per hour.

Some of these raging waters entered the Snake River Canyon at the site of the present Milner Dam, about twenty-five miles upstream. Some flowed out across the land north of the river in what is known as the Rupert Channel, which was carved into channeled scablands similar to those in central Washington. Water in the channel rejoined the river along a ten-mile stretch that includes Devils Corral and other lesser now-dry alcoves carved from the basalt.

Geologists think the peak flow lasted less than a month, but high flows ravaged the Snake River Canyon for more than a year. The erosive force remains evident in Devils Corral. As water flowed back into the canyon, it eroded the rim into a box canyon with a series of retreating semi-circular headwalls, leaving dry waterfalls twenty to fifty feet high, that stair-step down to the Snake River.

The only moisture on this autumn morning was a few drops of rain carried by the wind and leaving tiny craters in the dust. Even so, I can envision the violence of the Bonneville Flood—house-sized boulders tumbling along by churning, chocolate brown water. I can almost hear the deep, grinding rumbles and feel the earth shaking beneath my feet.

My reverie fades, and the only thing moving are sunbeams playing tag with low clouds scudding across the landscape.

From the upper end of Devils Corral, several trails lead down—some obvious, other you have to pick your way along carefully between boulders and openings in the basalt—to the first level maybe fifty feet below the rim. Below, a fox lopes past, stopping to check me out. But he takes off when he spots my four-legged hiking partner, pacing excitedly along the rimrock. The fox left only his tracks in the sand and his scent in the dog's nostrils.

The prints of small mammals, insects and weeds moved by the wind appear undisturbed in the sand. A pair of mule deer does with their nearly grown fawns graze below a twenty-foot cliff in a side alcove. My presence sends them out of sight around a ridge of crumbling basalt.

Half-way down the canyon, a vertical wall drops about thirty feet to a small emerald lake. Willows and a Russian olive grow in the reeds along the shore. A pair of cottontail rabbits scamper for their hidey-hole in the rocks. A squawbush splashes a blaze of orange across the rocks. Sagebrush grow taller than a man in some places along the sandy trail. Yellow-green and orange lichens and dark green mosses decorate basalt boulders with abstract shapes.

Where the canyon splits around a basalt monolith, a second vertical wall drops nearly one hundred feet, another of the now dry falls. Below, a clear, spring-fed pool eventually drains back into the Snake. On one side of the monolith is the stream that tumbles the final thirty feet down to the river, on the other side a dry stream leads west to the river as well.

In the brush, a red-brown mink slinks over the rocks to a secret place in the rocks. A chokecherry clings to a rock outcrop hanging over the steep, winding path down. Along the dry creek, white poplars glow with their yellow and gold fall plumage. Poison ivy spread a flourish of red among dark greens and browns of this riparian oasis.

Something rustles in the reeds; perhaps a muskrat. And that distant rumble? Is that the pounding of stolen horses' hooves? Or the rumple of an ancient flood? Alas, it's the semi-trucks on the interstate less than a mile away, bringing me back to reality.

November 23, 1995

The river in winter

It never gets too cold to go canoeing—too windy perhaps, but never too cold. As long as the river is open, calm winter days are perfect for a little quiet paddling. And calm days in southern Idaho are too rare to waste just because of a little cold.

Canoeing in winter has its own special attraction for me. Long-handled underwear, warm layers, hat and wool gloves—in case your hands get wet—are all a good idea; having an extra set of dry clothes and a blanket in a watertight bag also makes sense. A life-jacket is essential, but falling in the water is a bad idea when the temperature drops well below freezing.

On a windless winter day, the Snake River in southern Idaho near Twin Falls is the perfect place to do a little cold-weather paddling. A unique winter quiet settles into the canyon, the walls festooned with waterfalls arrested in time, and the banks generously dusted with snow.

Naked trees stand mute. The low winter sun rides the

south canyon rim. It gives little warmth, and leaves the air even colder in the shade below the canyon wall.

I have the river mostly to myself.

I work upstream under the highway bridge, and paddling against the current it is easy to stay warm. I try to keep my fingers out of the water—gloves help, but sometimes they make it harder to grip the paddle. The cold is sharp on my exposed cheeks; my breath comes out like smoke.

I slip beneath sheer rocks with their toes in the water. One looks like a profile of Abraham Lincoln. Basalt layers, stacked like a layer cake of ancient lava flows on top of rounded rhyolite rock, form the spectacular five hundred-foot canyon walls.

But all is not dead here, even in the depth of winter. Once while paddling this stretch, I watched a mule deer swim across the river. At first I thought it was a branch drifting with the current, but then I noticed it was moving across the current. And those were antlers, not a branch. I had no idea mule deer were such good swimmers.

The only sound was the gurgle of water stirred by the paddle. The canoe slipped silently through the water. A pair of red-tailed hawks circled above the canyon rim, and a red-shafted flicker disappeared into a hole in a snag. One of this year's fawns—nearly full grown—lapped cautiously from the river's edge.

With no wind, the water reflected the muted colors of late fall. Overnight rains blackened the trees trunks, and decaying leaves scented the air. Once erect reeds along the shore bent toward the water as if reaching for a drink. A few yellow leaves still clung to willows lining the river.

KER-SPLASH!

Something large and heavy startled me, but I couldn't tell what it was. A line of bubbles headed out from the shore, like a torpedo aiming for my starboard bow. My shaggy paddling partner sat up and looked at me with questioning eyes. He too had been startled.

Whatever it was, passed beneath me without incident.

It was probably a beaver, or maybe a muskrat. The water was too murky to see what passed beneath the hull. I circled back, but I didn't see it surface. The dog laid back down on his pad and sighed.

Startled by my approach, a belted kingfisher took off from a gnarled willow branch over the water. His rattling cry echoed along the river, and he lit on a branch farther upstream, a safe distance away, but scolding me all the way. A small blue and white bird with an oversize beak and an even bigger voice, the belted kingfisher lives mostly on minnows in shallow water near the shore. Overhanging branches form a perfect perch from which to prey on fish, and I have seen a kingfisher hover momentarily, drop on a fish and return to his perch to eat.

Some anglers mistakenly regard the bird as a competitor. But fish on the kingfisher's menu generally don't grow up to be game fish.

Other predators—including great blue herons, cormorants, muskrats, mink, otter and raccoon—are more serious rivals for the two-legged angler. I sometimes see one or two people fishing on the river, even on a cold morning.

A chorus of red-winged blackbirds rises from the cattails as I glide along the bank. I startle a coot preening in the reeds. It paddles furiously to get away, looking anxiously over its shoulder. A canyon wren flits in the willow brush. A pair of red-tailed hawks cut intersecting circles in the sky above the rim. A red-shafted flicker disappears in a hole high on a riverside snag.

The temperature drops another degree or two as I paddle back to the boat ramp and the warmth of the truck. I am continually amazed at the diversity of wildlife down here—even in winter.

Canoeing at this time of year requires an extra measure of care—to say nothing of an extra layer or two—but getting out on the water in the winter is well worth that effort.

December 21, 1995

Paddling memories

It's a sorry sight. I'm ashamed to admit it, but my canoe is encrusted with ice and snow.

Nature has conspired to keep me off the water lately windy and cold and the roads are terrible. So instead I sit and reminisce about other trips—past and future. Fresh in my mind was a trip late last summer to Pettit Lake in the Sawtooth National Recreation Area in central Idaho. I drove about three hours to the boat ramp, where I loaded tent and sleeping bag, camp stove and a cooler full of food and beer into the canoe—all carefully lashed in place. The extra weight, evenly distributed, made the canoe more stable, something I would appreciate greatly in the wind-whipped wave on my return trip.

I set out from the ramp and paddled out around a point of land. Along the shore I found a secluded flat spot in among the lodgepoles for a campsite. After setting up the tent and emptying the canoe, I spent the rest of the day exploring the lake at the foot of the Sawtooth Mountains. Back in camp, just before dusk, I fixed a simple dinner and relaxed with a beer.

A new moon rose over mirror-smooth water, and I couldn't resist. I lit a hurricane lantern and set it on a rock at the edge of the water by my camp to light my way back. I slid the canoe into the black water and paddled silently into void. My nearly imperceptible wake was the only disturbance on the water, like an umbilical cord connecting me with reality.

It was magical. I was transported to another dimension, suspended between heaven and earth—suspended between the sliver of moon and stars above and their reflections in the water. I floated in space, all sense of time and distance dissolved as I lay back in the canoe. Nothing stirred the unbroken surface of the water; no sound broke the silence and no thoughts interrupted this trance that blurred and then erased the distinction between time and space.

Time stopped, the moon disappeared behind the mountains, and stars grew more intense. I ceased to exist in the world, and simply became the world, the moon, the water, the shadows, the mountains, the Earth. My spirit united with the universe—I was the universe.

A faint noise like a dog barking in the campground about a quarter mile away finally broke the spell. I paddled back toward the kerosene beacon on the shoreline. I lay mesmerized in my sleeping bag a long time before fading off to sleep. A chipmunk trapped in my camp stove, woke me up early. The sun peeked over the mountains to the west through a lace curtain of lodgepole pines. Everything seemed brighter, smells more intense. The night before seemed like a dream, but its effervescence lingered. Reborn, I headed home.

Now, outside the wind is blowing, and it's a good time to get ready for new adventures, to drag out my gear to see what's missing, what needs repair. What was it that I just couldn't live without last year? For me, part of the fun of a canoe trip—or any sort of expedition for that matter—is the preparation, poring over maps, looking for just the right kind of rope, shopping for a new camp stove, making sure the sleeping pad hasn't developed any new leaks like it did last summer, drooling over outdoor catalogs, and making sure everything gets packed.

A friend set me thinking about a trip down the Smith River in Montana. Then again, the Henrys Fork has some nice quiet stretches. I might go there again. A few years ago I was in that area and explored the braided channels around Big Spring. I encountered my first moose and her calf.

I heard something like a washing machine with the lid left open when I got out of my tent on my first morning in camp. It was a mother moose and her calf in the willow thickets maybe twenty yards away. I ducked back to my truck for the camera, but I was already too late. They came crashing out of thick willow brush along the water, crossed the stream and headed off across a meadow. She was nearly black, and the calf was nearly grown. It was early September and they both looked fat and sleek and ready for winter.

Later that day, as I rounded a bend paddling a friend's canoe, I caught sight of an osprey dragging a bright red kokanee up on a sand bank. Its strong hooked beak had a solid grip, and its legs dug into the sand as it backed up, pulling its prize onto drier ground. I grabbed a handful of willows to hold myself in the gentle current and watched the bird as it began to tear into the fish. It glanced about nervously, but it wasn't bothered by my presence until the current forced the canoe onto some gravel that rattled against the wooden hull.

The fish was too big for the osprey to lift in its talons. The black and white bird weighed maybe three pounds, with a two-foot body and a five-foot wingspan. The fish looked like it weighed well over five pounds. With a strip of skin and flesh in its beak, the osprey lifted off and flew out of sight. I felt bad that I had disturbed its meal.

And people ask me what it is I like about canoeing on quiet (read, boring) waters. The fun is that when you slow down to watch and listen and feel, you notice what's going on around you, and sometimes that's some really amazing stuff.

February 9, 1996

Desert canyons

Vague tracks cross the rolling sagebrush sea. Out there somewhere before the distant mountains, the canyon of the Owyhee River's East Fork drops unexpectedly at your feet.

Sheer rock walls drop nearly a thousand feet to another world where silver ribbons twist between ocher walls, where lush vegetation along desert streams provide habitat for deer, elk and other wild creatures. The canyon rims shelter bighorn sheep, and thermal updrafts lift hawks and eagles. The peregrine falcon making a slow comeback from the edge of extinction has been sighted in this country.

After several hours of bad dirt roads, those vague, dusty tracks turn abruptly down into a side canyon. But years of erosion from infrequent desert rains have made it impassable. The only way down is on foot. The side canyon offers a steep access to the main canyon. The trail winds along the remains of an old wagon road disguised as a stream bed. It winds over talus and around rock outcrops. Then it opens into the great canyon, facing a sheer rock wall on the far side of the river.

Down here the rock walls of a burned out cabin remain—once part of a ranch, or perhaps it was a line shack, a place of refuge for cowboys far from the home ranch. But the grass hasn't seen a bovine for many years. It is tall and thick. The trash in the burned out shack gives evidence that it still offers refuge to passers-by—floaters on the river or hikers like myself.

The "ranch" is the site where California bighorn sheep were reintroduced into the East Fork canyon in the 1960s. This canyon offers prime habitat for bighorn sheep, with steep cliffs to escape predators and plenty of grass for forage. In the fall of 1963, Idaho Fish and Game trucks rattled down this road, hauling metal corral sections and nineteen bighorn sheep. The sheep were part of a gift of forty bighorns trapped near Williams Lake in British Columbia. The sheep were left in the corrals overnight to acclimate. But they kicked down the corral gates in the night, impatient to be free.

In 1965, nine more sheep from Williams Lake were released here, and ten more in 1966. This time, however, Fish and Game simply released them on the rim—they found their own way down much easier than the trucks. Today the canyon once again echoes with the crash of bighorn rams battering each other with their massive horns.

The herd has flourished here in this wild canyon country. It now is the largest herd of California bighorns in the United States, and it is the only herd healthy enough to provide transplant animals for other former sheep habitats. The history of sheep in this country is carved in the rocks here by ancient inhabitants thousands of years ago.

The Owyhee River canyon country in the southwest corner of Idaho, wild and unforgiving, whipped by freezing winds in the winter and scorched by the sun in the summer—is the largest piece of real estate in the lower 48 states without a paved road.

Some say the best way to see these canyons may be from a canoe, and the river offers one of the finest wilderness canoe trips in the country. This is the only other place in the country, except the Grand Canyon, big enough for a twenty-two day canoe trip.

I explored the grassy flat on the south side of the river and gazed in awe at the thousand-foot rock face rising out of the river's north side. I dipped my toes in the chilly water before starting back up the trail. The climb back out was strenuous. But that is exactly what has protected this extraordinary canyon. Only those willing to work hard for it, can get there. Anything that would make it easier would spoil the experience.

Back on the rim, I found a pair of speckled white eggs—cold to the touch, the mother long gone—apparently abandoned beneath a sagebrush. Survival comes hard out here in these desert canyons.

September 12, 1996

New boat, new adventures

The smell of new mown grass fills the air. Daffodils and tulips bask in the warm sunshine. Yard sale signs are popping up like mushrooms on lawns all over town. And the heating bill is down by half.

They're all sure signs that it's spring. And I have a brand new canoe. It was no easy task picking out a new boat. More than just money, it was a matter of what kind of canoeing I do most. Not all canoes are created equal. Each is designed for a specific kind of water. I wanted a boat that I can paddle by myself but big enough that I can take a friend along. It had to be light enough that I could lift it on the roof of the Jeep by myself. And I wanted a boat mostly for quiet water. So I got this fiberglass and wood canoe that is light and sturdy. It is more tippy than my old boat, but it is easier to paddle and maneuver. It slides through the water without so much as a whisper.

The new boat met its first challenge in the fast-moving Snake River. With the highest spring flows in a decade, the water rushed past the ends of the nearly submerged docks at the boat launch north of Twin Falls, in southern Idaho. Abundant snow in the mountains of western Wyoming, the headwaters of the Snake, means space must be made in the upstream reservoirs for when warmer weather comes to the high country and all that snow melts. The open floodgates create high waters downstream. Serpentine streaks of scum swirled in the swiftly moving stream. The morning sun was cold.

With the bow pointed slightly to the left, the current forced the boat sideways toward the opposite shore with each paddle stroke. Over here the swollen river has inundated the riparian woods. Like a river otter, I poke through the flooded forest, picking my way around submerged snags and brush. I imagined myself poling through a tangled mangrove swamp, alert for snakes and the floating logs that look like 'gators. But no alligators bellow in this imaginary bayou, the trees are only leafless willows, and my passage through the trees takes me back out into the current of the river.

The usual bird life was apparent. But this time of year a pair of ducks circle over a likely nest site, a pair of Canada geese honk. Meanwhile, from somewhere nearby a resident kingfisher, distant relative of Australia's laughing kookaburra, sent its call echoing across the canyon. I suspect it's hard to catch little fish in the current.

Upstream something bobbed in the water, a plastic bottle, riverbank refuse cast adrift by the high water. I struggled to keep moving against the translucent green current. When I rest my paddle, the canoe stops. If I hesitate longer, I begin moving backward. My reward came on the return trip when I relinquished control to the river. The only effort required was a few strong, well timed strokes to turn out of the current and into the calm water downstream of the docks.

The new boat passed the test. It maneuvered easily in the strong current, and I can load it easily by myself. And the unmarked hull is like a blank piece of paper, waiting for the scratches of adventures to come.

May 1997

Trophies in the mind

Sometimes being in the right place at the right time is not enough.

I was in Copenhagen recently on one of my regular visits to see my widowed mother. Desiring a break, I chanced to get away for an afternoon in the deer park just north of the city.

The park is bordered by city and suburbs, concrete, brick, rails and asphalt, but inside the fences nature still rules—mostly. A few of the gnarled oak trees are so old they have names. Some were seedlings eight centuries ago when the last of the Vikings still plied the waters visible to the east. I always spot herds of deer on my visits to the park, which was once the royal hunting preserve. An Italian Renaissance hunting lodge, built by a long-deceased Danish king, overlooks large meadows in the center of the park.

Walking trails familiar from my childhood, I followed

the bellowing of European elk, known as red deer but similar to their American cousins. The park also is home to herds of roe deer and the small Japanese sika deer. It was a cool October day, the beeches were just starting to turn yellow, and the sun played tag with fast moving clouds. In the shadows among the trees, I could hear the bellowing of a lone stag. I turned off the gravel path to try to get a better look.

Cutting through a thicket, I glimpsed the stag. He carried an impressive ten-point set of antlers. They must continually snag on the lower branches, I thought. Armed only with a 300 mm telephoto lens, fast color slide film and a motor-driven Nikon, I spent the next two hours stalking the grizzled veteran.

He was an old fellow. The rutting season was not yet over, and he didn't take kindly to my approach. When I neared he would bellow and paw the ground, lower his head and shake his rack as if I were one more challenger. I kept a respectful distance. If I was going to get a good shot, I'd have to be sneaky, and careful.

With the afternoon sun behind him, a picture in the shadows would not bring reasonable results. So I maneuvered to get the sun behind me. But when I moved around to the west, he moved into deeper shadows. Now a large swampy area kept me from moving directly through the trees to get on the other side of him.

He tantalized me several times with a stirring silhouette, standing between the trees as the sun broke through the scattered clouds. Good enough to make me fire off a few frames. But it was not the shot I wanted.

A light rain started.

I stopped and leaned against a tree to rest. I peeked

around the trunk. The stag hadn't moved. I checked the number of frames left on the roll in the camera. I had used thirty-four frames on a thirty-six-frame roll.

I peeked again. He was moving away.

Anticipating his movements, I worked myself into a position where the light would be right if he stepped into the open. The rain stopped. Sunlight broke through the overcast again, turning raindrops into diamonds against the dark green undergrowth.

And there he was, stopped in a shaft of sunlight, dark reddish brown, with some white low on his throat, and a grizzled back and muzzle. With his head thrown back and his chin up, he bellowed—perhaps frustrated with rejection of the hinds, or his inability to fight off younger stags, or the pesky human with the camera.

Bracing the long lens against the smooth bole of an old beech, I snapped one shot, bracketing the exposure, I snapped the last frame on the roll.

He stopped bellowing, eyed me suspiciously, and he seemed to sense that I was out of film, and that the game was over. The sun went behind a cloud, and he turned to graze a patch of grass and faded back into the shadows.

Back in the States, I eagerly awaited the results of my photographic hunt. Alas, the processor had run my slide film through the print film processor, ruining all my shots. I was bitter with disappointment. But all was not lost.

I still have the pictures in my mind, and I can't help but think they get better with age.

October 23, 1997

A matter of determination

Climbing that mountain was the toughest thing I've ever done, but it taught me the limit of my endurance and the depth of my determination.

In October of 1987, I took a trip to Mount St. Helens with the geology club at Western Washington University in Bellingham.

We carpooled to the foot of the mountain and made camp. The following day we drove to the trail head at about four thousand feet on the south flank of the volcano. On the way we made a side trip across an ash flow, a coarse gray carpet that literally cut through the landscape. Already the forest had begun to reclaim the barren stretch with a few struggling Douglas fir seedlings.

The trail started out pleasant, with an occasional peek through the trees at the forested slopes of the mountain. But that didn't last. We stopped for lunch at a level spot along a small creek. No blisters yet. I wore a pair of thin socks under my wool hiking socks, and the boots were broken in and in good shape. Antsy to get going, the group soon started up the mountain again. It was the last time I saw most of them, until I met them coming back down, several hours later.

After the lunch stop, we continued up the trail. It was four miles in and one mile up. The trail got steeper and less distinct as it climbed out of the trees. I struggled to keep up, but I soon fell farther behind until I was among the stragglers. The forty pounds of camera gear I carried didn't help. I clambered over and around the rocks—steadily up, always up. My legs were getting tired. The only people as slow as me were a guy with a knee brace, recovering from knee surgery, and his wife. I didn't care. It wasn't a race, and the trail was beautiful with increasingly spectacular views of the Cascade Mountains, Mount Adams and other large peaks.

At one point, I stopped to take a picture, and while changing lenses, I dropped one. It came to rest on the rocks about twenty feet below me. When I went after it, I lost my footing, and slid about ten feet down to a narrow ledge just above what was probably the only snow and ice left on the mountain. There was no way forward or back without crossing the treacherous patch of ice perhaps thirty feet wide. I took a chance. Scrambling and sliding, I made it across. But on the climb back up to the trail, I reached another dead end. The ledge I had been following narrowed to nothing. I was several yards to solid footing, and I couldn't go back. Hanging by my arms from a ledge, I reached for a foothold while slowly pulling my self along the ledge.

I made it to solid ground and got myself back up to the trail with all my camera gear intact, except for a broken lens filter and a few bruises and sore muscles. While resting from my ordeal, I spotted several of the geologists on their way back down. At least I knew that I was on the right trail to the summit.

The fall and climb out had taxed my legs, and I was facing loose gravel for the last thousand feet to the summit. With every step up, I slid a half step back. I wasn't giving up now; I could see the summit. My thighs were screaming, but I pushed myself upward, driven by determination. One step, rest; one step, rest. I forced my self to keep going.

I met one of the guides on his way down. He didn't want me high on the mountain after dark. I convinced him to let me get a few pictures in the golden light of sunset, and I promised not to be up there more than half an hour. He promised to wait for me.

With cramping thighs, I almost had to move my legs by hand. But I made the summit. I gazed down into the maw of the crater at least a mile across. It seemed impossible that there had ever been a mountain top here. Far below, I could see the beginnings of a new lava dome.

The view made me forget the pain in my legs.

To the northwest I could see the tumbled remains of the mountain top where it had slid into the Toutle River valley. To the northeast, Spirit Lake already was beginning to recover, and farther in the distance the massive fourteen thousand-foot bulk of Mount Rainier rose in the evening haze. The late sun caught the other Cascade volcanoes.

Then I noticed what I had taken to be smoke rising from the crater, was actually dust as pieces of the rim crumbled and slid into the crater—pieces just like the one I was standing on at the edge of a thousand foot drop. I backed away slowly.

I snapped a bunch of pictures and started back down. The going was a lot easier. One step, I slid twenty feet, mostly on my rear. I quickly got the hang of the glissade, and soon covered the distance that I only a short while earlier had struggled up one painful step at a time.

I rejoined the guide who had waited in the larger rocks below the gravel. I had overstayed my time at the summit, and he was grumpy in the quickly fading light.

It was dark by the time we got back to camp at the trail head. I was tired and sore, but satisfied that I had measured up—-if only barely.

I didn't join the revelry around the campfire that night. After eating, I unrolled my sleeping bag, crawled in and promptly fell asleep. I had climbed the mountain.

December 11, 1997

Finding peace in the wild

One of my favorite campgrounds is an out of the way spot on the west side of a man-made lake on the backside of Mount Baker in northwestern Washington.

The campground is about twelve miles north of the town of Concrete, and just southwest of the North Cascades National Park. The area was logged decades ago, but the loggers left a lot of old hemlocks, cedars and Douglas-firs in the campground. Vine maples and ferns grow around fallen giants between the campsites.

Across the lake at the north end, in the unlogged Noisy-Diobsud Wilderness Area, the trees are several hundred years old.

When the Upper Baker Dam was built and lake filled in 1959, the big trees on the east side became inaccessible. Years ago someone built a bridge across Baker Creek at the north end of the lake—no ramps, just a bridge. But the Forest Service has refused permission to build a road around the end of the lake. The Scott Paper Company— which once made advertising history by claiming its toilet paper was guaranteed not to cause hemorrhoids— proposed barging equipment across the lake to cut the big trees not included within the wilderness boundary.

One spring I paddled across the lake with some friends to hike up along Noisy Creek. The creek eloquently earns its name as it tumbles down among boulders and fallen trees. The down trees were so big I couldn't just step or jump over them; I had to climb belly first, then swing a leg up, to get over some of them. Normally when I walk in the woods, I can step over most of the fallen trees. We found what my friends thought must have been the biggest one—a venerable Douglas-fir, at least two hundred feet tall where the top had snapped off. It was more than thirty-six feet in circumference at shoulder height, and about eleven and a half feet in diameter.

These woods, on both sides of the lake, are home to a lot of wildlife. At various times I have spotted deer, elk, black bear and a variety of birds, both seen and heard. I never saw one, but I'm sure I heard a spotted owl one night. And some say there are grizzly bears roaming in the wilderness and the North Cascade Park above Baker Lake.

The lake once was much smaller. The Upper Baker Dam flooded the natural lake and the valley of Baker Creek when it choked off the creek in 1959. The reservoir today is about nine miles long. A pair of turbines in the powerhouse in the dam generate about one hundred megawatts of power.

Before the dam was closed and Baker Lake filled

for the first time, loggers were allowed to salvage the standing trees up to the high water line. In times of low water, however, many of the stumps they left become visible, high and dry. With the soil washed away from the roots, the stumps look like alien monsters stalking the banks of the reservoir.

The first time I went was in mid-March about ten years ago. I arrived in the afternoon and set up camp. Only two other campsites were occupied. And by evening the others had left to return to civilization. As the last car left, and I heard it fading away on the road, the realization began to sink in that there was no one else for miles around. The Baker Lake Resort a few miles down the road was still closed. The closest humans were in Concrete, twelve miles away.

The only sound was the bubbling of my dinner on the hissing camp stove. By dark I was completely alone. My only companions were my anxieties and the noises of the night. The sky was dark as it gets, with overcast and miles from any electric lights. I couldn't see a thing.

I was a little uneasy at first, and completely dependent on my own resources. Help was twelve miles away, and there was no phone—-this was long before the day of the cellular phone. I enjoy solitude, and I have never been afraid to be alone, but this was the first time I had spent a night so far out in the woods by myself. I crawled inside my flimsy nylon tent, and snuggled into my sleeping bag. I forced myself to lay back and listen to the night. I left the tent flap open to smell the moist forest air, fragrant with impending spring.

Small creatures crashed through the underbrush—- in my mind a raccoon sounded like a black bear.

Then I thought I heard a dog barking. That's odd, I thought. But as I listened, I could hear the pattern wasn't quite right for a dog. I finally recognized it as a spotted owl, probably in the old-growth forest across the lake.

I listened intently for it for a long time before I fell asleep.

January 8, 1998

Encounter with an owl

One day while driving across southern Idaho in the spring of 1999, I pulled off the lonely two-lane highway to stretch my legs and answer the call of nature.

I stopped on an abandoned side road between Carey and Richfield on my way across the vast expanse of broken lava of the Eastern Snake River Plain in southern Idaho.

From where I parked, I spotted a great horned owl, so I grabbed my binoculars for a closer look. That's when I spotted a second owl, sitting on a nest. Naturally curious, I wondered if any owlets were in that nest. The answer came when the second owl left the nest, and three woolly little heads jutted from the tangle of twigs. The sight was irresistible. I had to get a picture. I loaded some film in my camera. But, alas, I didn't have my long lens. I would have to try to sneak up as close to the nest as possible without alarming the adults. The task would put my best wait-observe-and-move stalking skills to the test.

I should have known better. I was setting myself up for an important lesson.

The adult owls weren't impressed with my stalking skills, nor did they approve of my approaching the nest. I heard a whole new range of noises that I didn't know owls could make—clicks and hisses and a bark that sounded like a small dog. All intended, I am sure, to drive me away.

I have often watched these great birds with fascination, but rarely had I been so close. I could have touched the nest from the ground. I know better than to disturb wildlife with young, but I couldn't suppress the urge to get a picture of the furry little nestlings.

I was wary of the big birds of prey. With distinctive ear tufts and piercing yellow eyes, the great horned owl— *Bubo virginianus*—is unmistakable. The adults range from eighteen inches to two feet tall, weighing up to three pounds, with a four-foot wingspan and powerful muscles and wicked talons. They are the biggest owl in southern Idaho. They make a respectable adversary for a human armed with nothing more than a 35 mm Nikon.

These owls typically nest in another bird's abandoned nest, or in a hollow tree or a cliff. The females usually lay three eggs in a clutch. They eat small animals such as gophers, lizards, rabbits, even skunks and the occasional grouse—and they are not above attacking any all-too-nosy photographers.

Keeping an eye on both birds wasn't easy, and at some point I knew I'd have to stand up and reveal myself to get a picture of the nest. I stayed close to the bole of a large cottonwood, as the two adults prowled the air, swooping close, hooting and barking as they flew. I was not deterred. I saw one owl land in a tree ahead of me and I had just seen the other one in a tree about fifty yards behind me, I stood up and clicked off several frames. All three of the big-eyed fluff balls looked straight into the camera. Not satisfied, I stretched on tiptoe. Just a few more frames. I was sure one owl was still in that tree behind me.

Now I was clear of the sagebrush cover, looking right into the nest. Just a couple more — WHAM! Something unheard, soft and sharp at the same time, like a feather pillow with rocks in it, hit me in the back of the head. It didn't hurt much at first, but it startled me and nearly bowled me over. I realized instantly that one of the adults had swooped in behind me without making a sound. But I got the message loud and clear. I clambered back through the brush and took refuge in the safety of my pickup truck. My hands fumbled for my keys and shook as I started the truck. I felt the back of my head, and my fingers came away bloody. The owl's talons had pierced my scalp. I put a paper towel on the wound, and turned the truck around with my left hand holding the towel.

As I drove away, I trembled with thoughts of how much worse it could have been, and I wondered whether I could get tetanus, or worse, from owl's talons. The bleeding soon stopped. The few scratches healed quickly, but the lesson stays with me still. I had learned emphatically about respecting wildlife and keeping my distance— especially when they have young. Adults don't think of their own safety when protecting their young. They will do whatever it takes to drive intruders away.

My brush with the owl was a bone-headed move,

but I was lucky. I could have been hurt worse. Still my curiosity and interest in the owls pulled at me. Several weeks later, I checked back on the owls to find three large, healthy-looking fledglings crowding the nest. This time I brought the long lens. I wore an old felt hat and kept at a respectful distance.

A hand absentmindedly strayed to some lingering scabs on the back of my head.

May 20, 1999

Feathered haven

The setting sun burnished trees, reeds and birds in the marshes on this summer evening. A flight of about a dozen white-faced ibis, their long legs stretched out behind and distinctive beaks pointing the way, coasted in to land on the mud. The elegant birds, with iridescent green and purple on their wings, moved along the water's edge. Their long beaks probed the mud for bugs—-what scientists call benthic invertebrates.

This year was unusual for the number of shorebirds in the Hagerman Valley on the Snake River in southern Idaho. Normally bird watchers would have to go to the American Falls Reservoir near Pocatello or to the shores of the Great Salt Lake to see such a variety and number of shorebirds. But even in an average year, the marshes and ponds of the Hagerman Wildlife Management Area is among the best places in Idaho for watching shorebirds and waterbirds. In 2000, however, Idaho Fish and Game, which runs the wildlife management area, had drained some of the ponds here to repair the dikes, bridges and water control structures. The work had exposed large mud flats that became a magnet for shorebirds.

Among the visitors were some infrequent visitors to Idaho that spend their summers in the Arctic and winter at the southern tip of South America. They often pass through, but rarely in such variety and number.

I spotted a great egret, several long-billed dowitchers with their improbably long, straight beaks, and a pair of graceful black-necked stilts with their trademark long pink legs. A small flock of western sandpipers scurried nervously nearby at the water's edge. None of them were birds one would associate with southern Idaho's arid high sagebrush steppe.

Interesting as the rare visitors were, what really makes this place special is the concentration of ducks, geese and other waterfowl in January and February. As many as sixty thousand ducks and more than four thousand Canada geese and other waterfowl winter here.

The Hagerman Wildlife Management Area, a partly artificial wetland about a hundred miles east of Boise, where the Snake River canyon widens into the Hagerman Valley, was established more than sixty-five years ago. In 1940, Fish and Game bought 423 acres of pasture along Riley Creek—what was once the Tucker Ranch became the Hagerman Valley Refuge. Since then, Fish and Game has added more land to what is now the 880-acre wildlife management area. Part of the area is a trout hatchery, and the rest is managed as wildlife habitat.

The area is hardly natural, however. This wildlife refuge consists of a series of natural creeks and ponds and seventeen man-made ponds and wetlands on a flat bench in the Snake River Canyon above the Snake River. Water for the hatchery and the ponds comes from several springs and from Riley Creek, which also is spring-fed. Mild winters in the protected Hagerman Valley and spring water at a near-constant 58 degrees, keeps the area ice-free in most winters and makes it a powerful lure for waterfowl.

The open water makes the area popular with ducks, geese and other water birds in winter. The area also is one of the few spots in southern Idaho where you can watch shorebirds normally seen on ocean beaches, as they stop to rest on their annual migrations. With so many birds in the area, it's not surprising that owls, hawks, ospreys, bald and golden eagles prowl the area. The area is a pleasant place for a walk, but the grass is tall and ticks are abundant at times so long pants are a good idea.

The reeds and brush also are alive with red-winged and yellow-headed blackbirds and a variety of upland songbirds—to say nothing of small mammals, such as beaver, muskrat and mink. In the woods at the edge of the marshes I have found western wood-pee-wee, eastern kingbirds, yellow warblers and nighthawks. Kingfishers are regular residents, and great blue herons stand like fixtures ever ready to spear a meal in the shallows. Cormorants drape themselves to dry on old utility poles rising from the water.

In the late afternoon, as I walked the road atop one of the levees that form the ponds, I noticed a strange iridescent-green sheen on one of the ponds ahead. Could it be grass or reeds kept green by the unfrozen water? I set up the spotting scope with a clear view of the pond still almost half a mile away, and zeroed in on the wondrous and mysterious phenomenon.

All I saw were ducks. Thousands of mallard drakes. A virtual carpet of ducks at the far end of the pond. Just the right combination of low, winter afternoon sun shining on distinctive green heads of thousands of ordinary mallard drakes created this marvelous sheen.

August 24, 2000

Reflections

Woodshed, Stanwood, Washington

It's the journey that counts

Apowerful wind out of the south blew the rain along
the beach. Raindrops stung my face, and I could
not keep my eyes open facing that gale. The sand was
gray; the low clouds were gray; and the foam-flecked
ocean was gray. But the beach at Ocean Shores on
the Washington coast was speckled with bright green,
red and yellow rain gear. Several dozen clam diggers,
seemingly oblivious to conditions, had come to dig
the elusive razor clam. And timing is everything when
pursuing these tasty bivalves. It has to be in the hours
just before low tide, when the tide is still going out—
regardless of the weather.

I learned that there is much more to digging razor
clams than just bringing home a sackful of tasty clams—
heck, you can buy them in the store. A big part of digging
razor clams is in the digging itself—enduring cold, rain,
wind, dark of night, to pursue the wily bivalves. It's

digging furiously after a six-inch clam that can move though wet beach sand faster than most people can dig, getting soaking wet in the bargain, and then laughing about it later. I know some people might disagree with me, but—like a lot of other things in life—I think the clams taste better if you dig them yourself and if you suffer a little to get them. It's not even about digging clams; it's about being out there.

It's something so intangible that if I hadn't experienced it myself, I might not believe it. It was a lot like a day I spent on the Satsop River with a steelhead fishing guide. Setting off in an open drift boat on a rainy January morning on a river on the Olympic Peninsula might seem crazy to some. But it also is part of the lure of the outdoors and the pursuit of the elusive winter steelhead that run up the short wild rivers of the Olympic Peninsula.

The weather can be miserable here in winter. So I had serious misgivings as I pulled off U.S. Highway 12 about an hour west of Olympia, Washington. Thick winter clouds, heavy with rain, sagged just over the tree tops. Fishing guide Jim Tuggle waited for me in the muddy parking lot on the left bank of the Satsop River.

"Call me Tug," he grinned, leaning on the gunwale of his gray fiberglass drift boat, in which we would spend the better part of the day pursuing the wily steelhead.

"Great day for fishing," he predicted with a face full of professional optimism.

The day was memorable, not for the fish we didn't catch, but simply for a great day in the outdoors.

The Satsop River runs cold and clear out of the heavily forested southwest side of Washington's waterlogged Olympic Mountains, hiding somewhere in the overcast.

The river joins the Chehalis River that runs into Grays Harbor and then the Pacific Ocean. Big feisty steelhead run up the Satsop to spawn in the clean gravels of tree shaded riffles in the upper reaches of the river and its tributaries.

I followed Tug's rig onto the two-lane East Satsop Road, windshield wipers working overtime. We threaded our way north past farmsteads, weekend cabins and woods of western hemlock, western red cedar and Douglas fir, with blackberry brambles and vine maples in the undergrowth. We stopped and left my vehicle at the take-out, and continued north. After about 12 miles we reached Schafer State Park on the East Fork of the Satsop.

We stowed our gear beneath the boat's meager foredeck—the only dry spot on board—and manhandled the boat down a pot-holed, dirt and cobble ramp. Rain hissed on water transparent as a campaign promise. As I bent to the task of launching, large raindrops off a drooping hemlock branch found the gap between my hat and rain jacket with laser-guided accuracy. Cold trickled down between my shoulder blades.

Then, after a tenuous moment suspended between slippery bank and unsteady boat, we slid into the current that turned us downstream. Tug at the oars scanned the water for likely steelhead hiding spots. He nosed under the bare branches of Randy's Tree—a dead alder that leaned out over the river and bore the marks of an earlier encounter with a drift boat—and tossed out the anchor, letting the current hold the boat. Tug pulled out a fly rod and tied on a salmon hook festooned with neon green and orange yarn. He cast across the current and let the lure sink.

"You've got to present it to them on the bottom," said Tug, who spent twenty eight years as a game warden with the Washington Department of Wildlife. He now works as a fishing guide—getting paid for what he loves to do—in Washington and Alaska.

He reeled in and cast again, trying for just the right spot. More than anything, winter steelhead fishing takes good rain gear and lots of patience.

"Steelhead is a fish of a thousand casts," Tug said with unflagging enthusiasm. And a gray day makes for better fishing.

Steelhead are large rainbow trout that, like salmon, migrate to the ocean to mature for a couple of years, returning to spawn in their native stream. They always face upstream and seek cover along the bottom, he noted. They prefer water four to ten feet deep, moving at a fast walk. Anglers usually find them in slower water above a riffle, resting after passing through fast water.

When they hit, they hit hard, he said.

He pulled up the anchor and steered us back into the current. Around the next bend, the river disappeared under a recent deadfall rising taller than a man, blocking the channel in the middle of the river. The alternatives didn't look good—and there wasn't much time to decide— wait too long and the current would decide for us. We picked a shallow, bottom-scraping side channel that required a push.

Gravel crunched under the hull. I stepped in the shallow water to boost the boat over the bar and got my boot full of water for my effort. But we were free, drifting toward the next good steelhead spot. The anchor went over the transom again; the fly rod sang through the wet air; water gurgled along the hull; rain pelted our heads.

Cast followed cast. Nothing.

Mists rose from the trees on the hillsides along the river like ragged bits of cloud caught in the branches. The air carried the spicy clove scent of fecund Northwest Coast forest. The rain let up a little, as a juvenile bald eagle turned its head to check us out as he flapped by and disappeared into the trees.

Tug felt a pull on the fly line. He expected at least a twenty-pounder to come flashing and leaping from the water, every ounce fighting like a demon. They're exciting to catch, and they're very good eating. But there's more to it.

Alas, it was only a log on the bottom. Tug freed his lure and tried again. No luck.

The anchor came up again. He remembers catching a twenty-four-pound steelhead on a February day about twelve years earlier at a spot just a little farther downstream. It was the biggest steelhead he's ever caught on the Satsop.

Below the confluence where Decker Creek enters from the west, the anchor went in again. Perfect steelhead habitat, he said. Moving water more than four feet deep, places to hide and places to rest. But after a dozen fruitless casts, we moved on.

He dropped anchor again where the Middle Fork of the Satsop entered from the right. Here the river gets brawnier, wider, and the anchor holds only tenuously in the cobble. This is where someone else caught a thirty-pounder, he said.

Tug dipped a battered aluminum coffee pot in the river and set it on a propane burner, hissing and glowing red in the bottom of the boat between us. While it boiled, he passed out some home-smoked Puget Sound oysters. After a few minutes, he poured the boiled river water. Instant soup never tasted so good.

We swapped stories and cursed the rain. Maybe it wasn't such a good day for steelhead after all, he confessed as the bottom of the boat ground onto the rough cobble at the take-out. He apologized for not showing us any fish—but hey, steelhead are fickle and unpredictable.

"There's only three thousand steelhead that live in this river. They'll come back if you just let them spawn," he said. Catching a twenty-pound fish would have been good, he admitted. But that's not the only reason he goes fishing.

"A lot of reason I do this is the social stuff," he said. He enjoys sharing time with clients and friends, telling stories, swapping bad jokes, enjoying a cup of warm soup on a cold rainy day.

As much as I enjoy eating freshly caught steelhead, I too got something better. A day outdoors in good company is always worthwhile, even on a wet, cold day. And I never head out expecting anything more than I get. That way I'm never disappointed, and I sometimes learn something.

Though we didn't catch any fish, there was enough scenery, sodden as it was in the winter rain, enough camaraderie and enough intangibles to make it a full and satisfying day. For those hours, I managed to forget all the petty pursuits that normally take up my time. We had no destination. Being on the river was our destination.

There was no place I would have rather been.

Too often, I too have lost sight of everything but the destination, missing the details that make up life. But it's all those details, including being cold, wet, tired at the end of the day, that make it all worthwhile.

After all it's a poor adventure that is measured only in what you catch or kill.

January 19, 2003

Daydreams

My canoe, normally dark green, has a patina of dust that records the various wood working projects I have undertaken in my garage this past year.

None of those projects included paddling.

I'm writing this during a January snow storm in Idaho in 2009. I quit the newspaper business at the end of December 2005 and returned to Idaho. Now I'm contemplating some of my former haunts and exploring some new ones. I've had some exciting outings since taking a new job with a government agency in Boise— including trapping gray wolves with a couple of wildlife biologists. And last year it was a jet boat trip up Hells Canyon.

Earlier today, I took advantage of the new fallen snow and spent the morning skiing in a local park. It is close by and there aren't a lot of people there this time of year—especially not on a Sunday morning. We watched a dozen or so American widgeons follow a mallard drake and hen to a crab-apple tree full of cedar waxwings. The ducks were going to feast on the crab apples the waxwings were knocking on the ground. Who said ducks are dumb? There are lots of ducks in this park and huge flights of Canada geese. A couple of bald eagles flapped by, and a Cooper's hawk found a handy roost in a leafless oak. The resident great blue heron was installed at the edge of a bit of open water, standing like a statue waiting for lunch to show itself.

It was wet though. Just above freezing so the soft snow melted on contact with hat, coat and gloves. The clouds hung low over the nearby foothills, and I couldn't help but think all that snow would soon become potential canoeing water. Which brings me to the subject at hand. Canoeing water is a littler harder to find here—that is there isn't a lot close by. There is a couple of small lakes nearby—ponds really. The Boise River is inviting, but it requires a shuttle. I have to admit that I got spoiled living in Twin Falls. The Snake River launch to an excellent stretch was only twenty minutes from my house. The perfect spot. Flat water, though moving, stretched a couple of miles upstream of the launch. Perfect for a morning outing or a quiet evening paddle. Then the lazy current helped on the way home. Unless of course that pesky west wind kicked up.

Since moving here I have shifted my focus—canoeing here will require a longer trip and actual planning. So I have been poring over maps to find suitable places for day trips and weekend trips. I've had my eye on Deadwood Reservoir in the mountains north of Boise. Last summer my plans to go there were smoked out when more than two million acres of forest were on fire, and one of those fires had closed the road.

But I now live close enough to work to ride a bicycle most days. And that has been a whole new set of outdoor adventures—only a few involved flat tires. Most involve the Boise Greenbelt, which runs along the Boise River all the way through the city and makes up most of my daily ride. On my way I encounter a variety of birds and wildlife. The ducks change with the seasons, winter has brought common goldeneyes, hooded mergansers, common mergansers, buffleheads and American widgeons along with the resident Canada geese. Occasionally I encounter a red fox, once I saw a pair. One day I watched a fox eat a gopher, not fifteen feet from where I stopped my bike. I regularly see mule deer and mink—once I nearly ran one over when it crossed the bike path in front of me. I also see kingfishers, bald eagles, cormorants and great blue herons.

One day while I stopped to pump up a low tire, I watched a male goldeneye do his dominance display. He would bob his head a few times then throw it back and emit an unduck-like gurgling sound. Back on the trail, I rode into the orange glow of sunrise through a lace curtain of bare winter trees and morning river mist. A placid stretch of river reflected the glow. A chorus of Canada geese serenaded my ride.

Sometimes even a flat tire can have its rewards.

January 2009

About the author

Photo by Sue Nass

Niels Sparre Nokkentved lives with his wife in Boise, Idaho. His writing and reporting have earned him several awards for investigative journalism. Born in Denmark, he grew up in western Canada and northern Illinois. The Vietnam War and the U.S. Navy brought him to California 1968. After the service he traveled extensively before moving to Washington to attend college. He earned bachelors degrees in journalism and environmental studies from Western Washington University. Since 1986 he has written about natural resources and environmental issues and the outdoors for newspapers in Idaho, Washington and Utah. This is his third book.